Laughter at the Door

FOR JOCELYN

Laughter
at the Door

A Continued Autobiography

GEOFFREY TREASE

MACMILLAN

SBN: 333 16811 9

First published 1974 by
MACMILLAN LONDON LTD
London and Basingstoke
Associated companies in New York
Dublin Melbourne Johannesburg and Madras

Printed in Great Britain by
WESTERN PRINTING SERVICES LTD
Bristol

Set in Monotype Bell

Acknowledgement

The author is indebted to Sir George Trevelyan, Bt,
for kind permission to quote letters from the late Sir
Charles Trevelyan, Bt.

Contents

Lo, life again knocked laughing at the door!
The world goes on, goes ever, in and through,
And out again o' the cloud.

Robert Browning: *Balaustion's Adventure*

CHAPTER ONE

The Waiting Time

I KNEW that I had to go on writing. All my life I had had to write. Even a world war could not stop the itch.

So that first day I opened a new Woolworth notebook. I had no work in progress. I had just finished rewriting and expanding a play, *Colony*, which had been running for the past five weeks at the left-wing Unity Theatre and was due to open in the West End within a fortnight. I had signed the new contract only two days ago, but it looked doubtful now if the document had any meaning. A little self-consciously I headed the first page of the notebook with what could be safely assumed to be a historic date. '1939, Sept. 1st,' I wrote. 'We heard the news in the broadcast bulletin at 10.30 a.m.'

I suppose I had been expecting it, off and on, for the past twelve years. My pacifist phase had begun in the Sixth Form and lasted until Hitler's accession made me think again. In my bachelor Bloomsbury days I had joined, briefly, the Independent Labour Party and more recently I had belonged to the orthodox Labour Party, though myself far from orthodox and a follower of men like Stafford Cripps and Aneurin Bevan, then in the wilderness. My brash idealism had been fortified by a summer in Russia, spending the frozen Soviet royalties on my first children's books. It had been a mellow season, 1935, with the worst hardships of the Five-year Plan only a memory and the Stalinist purges not begun. Non-party 'progressives' were cultivated, it was the age of the People's Front, and there were welcoming smiles even for enlightened Tories like the Duchess of Atholl. And how could I myself see no merit in a country which sold a hundred thousand copies of my *Bows Against the Barons* while in Britain the sales stood at two or three thousand?

I have never been, like so many writers of my generation, a
Communist or even pressed to become one. But I knew Com-
munists – including some I did not recognise as such – and
some of the superficial Marxism rubbed off on me. The political
side of me had long accepted the dogma that capitalism made
war sooner or later inevitable.

There was, however, another side of me. The struggling
author, full of personal dreams, with a first novel just published
after several disappointments and now this play accepted for
the West End, could not help hoping against hope that somehow
ordinary life would go on. 'The news that the bombs were
actually dropping in Poland crushed that hope,' I wrote in my
notebook.

I am glad I still have it. Its jottings, however banal and
sometimes embarrassing, remind me of how I felt then, and save
recollection from the distortion of hindsight. We had steeled
ourselves for apocalyptic horror. H. G. Wells's film, *The Shape
of Things to Come*, had shown us the heavens opening and the
population choking in a sea of poison gas. The Government had
endorsed the prophecy with a wholesale distribution of gas-
masks and its plans to evacuate the cities.

Yet that first morning nothing happened. Berkshire spread
green and gold outside my window, the vast cornfield stretching
to Radley College, the hazy woods of Nuneham across the
unseen Thames, timeless and peaceful. Only the insistent radio
broke the illusion. On and on went the bulletins and announcements, the soothing B.B.C. voices. Everything was in hand. No
panic. Do as you are told, do nothing until you are told. The
ship might be sinking, I thought grimly, but it would be quite
all right if we all stood at our allotted boat-stations and did not
look through rails at the rising sea.

I dared not miss the announcements. I was enrolled in the
Officer Cadet Reserve, humblest of all such registers, since my
military qualifications did not go beyond the War Office Certifi-
cate A I had gained at school. I had no idea when, if ever, I
should be told to report. I never was.

Marian carried on with the housework. Routine had to
continue and Jocelyn was not yet three. At any time we might
have to receive 'evacuees' – we must not call them 'refugees'.

They had been pouring out of London in trainloads, apparently, since first light.

Ours came early in the evening. A pathetic little group clustered under the chestnut-tree at the bend in the road, a dozen or more little boys, three or four little girls, two armleted girl helpers in their teens, and several motherly local ladies trying to sort things out. It was rather like a benevolent slave-market. No prior arrangements had been made, but most of the neighbours were there to offer hospitality. We were assigned the two helpers, friends who did not want to be separated, and both confusingly named Lily. Privately (and with a certain ignoble relief) I thought we had been rather lucky to get the Lilies. I had not that passion for children's society at close quarters which most people expect a children's writer to feel. Nor (having once lived and worked for a period in the East End) had I any sentimental illusions about the children there. Though the Lilies were only about sixteen it should be easier to share our little house with them. Even the fact that we should be paid the adult rate of billeting allowance for them – small enough, but more than the child's – was something to be thankful for. Despite all the flattering press-notices of recent weeks, we were still struggling along on a microscopic income.

Later, we had cause to wonder whether the gathering of the Lilies had been quite such a good idea.

The next morning, Saturday, we woke to find ourselves alive and Britain not yet at war with Germany. The Lilies, amiable girls, made themselves thoroughly at home. Marian cooked sausages for breakfast. The taller Lily stretched across the table and speared one from my plate. 'I like 'em well done like this one,' she remarked approvingly. Outside, all along our tree-fringed country road, the children were exploring, greeting each other, and comparing notes. 'Jer know where our Doris lives?' 'Yus.' 'Wot number?' 'Don't know the number – know the name.' Two small boys came clattering, their boots seemingly shod with iron. One had his paws cupped tight together. 'Got a little frog, mister! Gonna ask Mrs Nichols if we can put 'im in 'er pool.'

Sunday brought Neville Chamberlain's broadcast announcement that we were now at war. It only temporarily broke the intensifying atmosphere of anticlimax. While two thousand German aircraft bombed Poland and fifty-four divisions overran the western half of her territory, nothing much seemed to be happening elsewhere. We know now that it took six weeks to move the first four British divisions across the Channel and that even six months later, as Churchill wrote, 'We were not of course at any point in contact with the enemy.' Later generations, brought up to think of the Second World War in terms of Dunkirk and D-Day, the Battle of Britain and the Coventry blitz, cannot imagine the emotional deflation of those early months.

That September was dry and sunny. Never had our loop of the Thames valley looked more mellow. Westwards, over Rush Common, the sunsets hung behind the black elms with all the splendour that Arnold described in 'Thyrsis'. Our house might itself be prosaic, a typical inexpensive 1936 product, to which we had moved (helped by a second mortgage from my mother) just before Jocelyn was born. But it bordered a region soaked in poetry. A stroll took us to 'the skirts of Bagley Wood'. We were only a few miles from the 'warm green-muffled Cumner hills', 'the stripling Thames at Bablock-hithe', and 'that sweet City with her dreaming spires'. In gloomier moments I sometimes felt like the Scholar-Gipsy, that seventeenth-century dropout who

came, as most men deem'd, to little good,
But came to Oxford and his friends no more.

In my case, however, I returned to Oxford quite often, as our nearest big town, and Blackwell had published my boys' adventure story about the start of the East India Company, *In the Land of the Mogul*, the first of a long series of books I was to write for them. It was my friends who came to Oxford no more. It was ten years since I had thrown up my classical scholarship at Queen's, burning my boats for the first time. My friends of that period were scattered. If even one had stayed as a don, my life at Abingdon would have been less lonely.

Arnold associations meant nothing to the Lilies, who cared little even for the halcyon weather outside, preferring to stay in their bedroom and play cards. At least this kept them out of the sitting-room during the day, when it had to do duty as my study, so that they did not disturb the writing I was soon struggling to resume. It did sometimes cross my mind that, as London County Council 'helpers', they might have some responsibility for all the little boys and girls in the neighbouring houses, now running wild. It did not cross the minds of the Lilies. Once I did encounter a vague-looking stranger, a teacher possibly, and inquired if someone might not organise something, for the field behind our house was ideal for rounders and the hedgerows glittered with blackberries. He rebuked me for so irresponsible a suggestion. The children must not congregate together. They might be suddenly machine-gunned from the air. So the Lilies continued their endless cardplaying upstairs and the children, bored and aimless, congregated just the same.

It was not long before we discovered that our guests had brought others with them. They had nits in their hair, which they soon shared with Jocelyn. Rage, despair and revulsion seized us. Marian battled grimly, equipped with special comb and chemical preparations. Meanwhile, as no bombs had fallen, the homesick children were trickling back to Millwall. First one of the Lilies departed, then the other. The nits took longer to go. But the second girl's departure was sufficient cause for celebration. We opened a bottle of sherry, a rare extravagance in those days, and drank to the restoration of home life, civilisation, and all the other things we were supposed to be defending.

Were we? Sometimes one wondered. Poland was down and out. In the west, between the massive fortified lines, scarcely a shot had been exchanged. As winter came, people talked more and more of the phoney war and the likelihood that even now Chamberlain and Daladier would negotiate a peace. I myself had received no word from the War Office. Had I been of a truly martial temperament I could have rushed, as some did, to enlist in the ranks. But there was not much of the 1914 spirit about and even a Rupert Brooke might have hesitated. The Government had us all docketed and would call us when wanted.

Most people could carry on 'business as usual' and make a virtue of it. For a writer it was not so easy. It was six years since I had burnt my boats for the second time, marrying on my

twenty-fourth birthday and simultaneously embarking on the
risky career of a free-lance. They had been six years of struggle.
By 1939 I had established something like a beachhead. I was
no longer just a writer of children's books. In July I had appeared as a novelist with *Such Divinity* and, a week later, as a
playwright. But the beachhead was obliterated almost as soon
as it was won. The closing of the theatres killed the West End
prospects of *Colony*: even when they reopened, it was too controversial for wartime performance, and after the war its heresy
had become orthodoxy and it was out of date. And when the
bombing did start in 1940 all remaining stocks of the novel
went up in flames.

That misfortune at least lay hidden in the future. In the last
months of 1939 'business as usual' meant, for me, writing a
second novel and earning what few guineas I could from minor
journalism, where already paper-rationing had reduced the
market. So I got down to my second light satirical novel, which
George Orwell was later to praise very generously and for
which Chapman & Hall promised me an advance of twenty-five
pounds – on publication. Till then, as we had to eat, I scraped
the barrel. A guinea from *Tribune*, a guinea from a Birmingham
Sunday newspaper, three guineas from the *Boy's Own Paper*. . . .
Things were as grim as they had been in our first year. And this
was the seventh.

It was a hard winter. I used to trudge through the snow into
a little spinney and drag back dead branches for the fire. Each
bough had an outer skin of ice. I can still hear the squeak of the
saw, see the ice-splinters fly before the blade reached the bark.

We were not of course romantically destitute. The public
tends to imagine that all authors either starve in garrets or earn
so much that they cannot afford to live in Britain. Ninety-nine
per cent come actually betwixt and between. I was just near
the lower end. We ate, very occasionally we drank, we were
not in rags or in debt, we could afford simple pleasures and
enjoyed them with zest.

Jocelyn, now three, cheerful and gregarious, needed more
contemporary company, so she started at a small private school
in the middle of Abingdon. Before getting down to the day's
work I would take her to the bus-stop, a lively little sprite in

red pixy-hood and olive-green leggings, clutching her penny in one red-mittened paw and, in the other, her miniature wicker basket with its single apple for mid-morning break. Then, handing her aboard to welcoming senior school-fellows, I went home to my typewriter.

Concentration might be easier, with only Marian and myself in the house, but I missed the old routine of the after-breakfast walk with Jocelyn. Usually we had made for the duck-pond beside Radley church, a mile or so of leaf-hung by-road, skirting the vast cornfield. We had the pushchair for when she tired – or for her to push, herself, in wild zigzags across the road, if she felt unduly energetic and helpful. I was very content that our child had been a daughter. Small girls were a fascinating novelty, for I had had no sisters. Apart from the delight that fathers commonly find in daughters, I had a kind of practical, professional bonus in this belated opportunity to study the young of the opposite sex. It helped that she was articulate. Her teacher, commenting on the Christmas play at the end of term, said, 'I've never *seen* such a bored angel.' 'Bored?' echoed Marian. 'Yes – she wanted to be a shepherd. The angels had nothing to say. They just sang.'

In those quiet winter mornings I began *Cue for Treason* for Basil Blackwell's 'Tales of Action' series, to which Cecil Day Lewis and Rex Warner had already contributed. One motive for writing juvenile books is to communicate your own enthusiasm. In this story two loves combined to give it life, the Elizabethan theatre and the Cumbrian landscape. I knew Cumberland only from brief walking tours, but I was steeped in Shakespeare and Marlowe. I had acted in them at school, devoured them in print, and seen every possible production from the aged Benson on tour to the young Gielgud at the Old Vic. Of theatrical history, as of social history generally, I knew little. In those days I had none of the books on everyday life, costume, arms, architecture and other essential background knowledge that cram my shelves now. I found one useful volume on the Elizabethan theatre in the library of the Oxford Union. I had a one-inch map of Cumberland and Bradley's *Highways and Byways*, in which I learned of the Cumbrian 'statesmen', or independent small farmers, with whose struggle against an enclosing landlord the tale begins. I was so ignorant that in the original edition I made him a baronet, twenty years before that rank was created.

Most readers are not, of course, pouncing pedants, though the observant child will detect such errors with immense glee. But, while there is no possible excuse for avoidable inaccuracy, vitality is far more important, and to the end of his days the author must be on his guard against losing it. The more research he does, the more he surrenders to the enchantment of authentic detail, the more he risks slowing down the action. When he finds himself thinking, 'This is marvellous, this is much too good to leave out!' it is time to ask himself, 'But where – *essentially* – does it fit in?' The writer's personal enthusiasm may be the motive power, but it must be controlled like any other engine.

It would be dull, and dangerous, to 'cater' deliberately for the children's own supposed tastes. These are hard to predict even in one's own country and impossible in a remote one. Many years after the writing of this Cumbrian story I met a publisher's representative newly back from west Africa. 'Do you know which of your books they all wanted?' she said. '*Cue for Treason*.' 'Oh,' I said, 'that'll be because I brought in Shakespeare – he's universal.' 'No,' she answered. 'It was because your first chapter has a riot over a land-boundary, and then your heroine runs away from a forced marriage. They said the book was about things that everybody was familiar with.'

I worked on this story in the bleak early months of 1940, and perhaps it gained gusto from the imaginative escape it offered me from the depressing atmosphere of the phoney war. It was much the best children's book I had so far written. Twenty years later Margaret Meek suggested, most generously, that 'with it a new era in the adventure story opened'. If so, the new era very nearly closed again, for by autumn the bombs had begun to fall in earnest. One delayed publication. Then, when I was just basking in the glow of excellent reviews, another destroyed the entire unbound stock in the warehouse. It was more than a year before Blackwell could reprint, but meanwhile the book was taken in America by Vanguard, and I knew its survival was assured. My two adult novels were similarly bombed out of print, but for them there was no resurrection.

While writing *Cue for Treason* I had to think hard about our

finances. There was no word from the Officer Cadet Reserve. I
could see no way to earn more by writing. I was thankful to
pick up a few weeks' work collecting sample reports for the
British Institute of Public Opinion. Often, that January and
February, I had to quit my desk, deserting Peter Brownrigg
and Kit Kirkstone in some dire Elizabethan plight, and pedal
round the frosty byways of Radley and Abingdon, interrogating
the appropriate age and income groups. When that ceased, I
had to think again. In the first seven months of war I had earned
from all sources less than a hundred pounds.

What could I do until my army call-up? For one year, before
we were married, I had taught in a small private boarding-
school. If I had managed to get that job, without a degree, in
the competitive era of the economic depression, surely I could
get one now, as the younger schoolmasters were drafted into
the forces? It would probably mean separation, for such jobs
were mostly resident and without married quarters, but it was
not likely to be for long. And if my call-up was slower than
expected we could perhaps arrange something. I applied to a
scholastic agency and unearthed my old testimonial.

I was quickly accepted, without even an interview, by a small
preparatory school on the seaward side of the Lake District. It
was a resident job, the pay reasonable. I could send most of it
to Marian until I found some way for her to join me.

Hastily I rubbed up my elementary subjects, planned some
lessons, prepared my mind for the transition to a world of
conventions I had long discarded. I had better, I felt, forget that
I had written *Bows Against the Barons*, been to Moscow, and
chaired the Abingdon branch of the Labour Party.

Thirty years later an old pupil showed me the school pros-
pectus for 1938, which I had never seen before:

Boys are prepared for Eton and the larger Public Schools.
The School is frankly designed for the sons of country
gentlemen, and of others who believe whole-heartedly in
English country life, and in riding and other manly outdoor
pursuits. There is fox-hunting, otter-hunting, beagling, sea-
bathing, mountain-climbing, and occasional fishing. The
male teaching staff is composed entirely of Oxford and

Cambridge men, with good degrees and successful experience.

It was lucky that I had not read this document when, on 1 May, I started my long train-journey to the North. It would not have raised my spirits, and they were already low enough.

CHAPTER TWO

Bannermere

THE school was at Gosforth, three miles inland from Seascale, a station on the coastal line which branched off at Carnforth and meandered round, via Barrow-in-Furness and Norman Nicholson's Millom (as we think of it now) to the Solway and Carlisle. In stretches a poetic, panoramic route. Whatever my other feelings when I used to travel it there was always a temporary lifting of the heart as I saw the fells rearing up inland and the Irish Sea glittering away to the fretwork silhouette of the Isle of Man.

Cumberland has always meant something special to me. Though my love of mountains was born in north Wales I feel – as an Englishman, I suppose – much more at home in Cumbria. I had been there only three times, camping with a school-friend, walking alone, and walking with Marian, when a rucksack dropped on Striding Edge had helped me to imagine, years later, a grimmer episode in *Cue for Treason*, when I wrote: 'But he bounced sideways and went rolling down into the mist-brimmed gulf of Nethermost Cove. He was lost to sight almost immediately, but for ages, as it seemed, I could hear the trickle of scree, like shingle on the beach, following him as he rolled over and over.' If the writer of adventure stories has enough imagination, he can make a minimum of actual experience go a long way.

That evening in 1940, though, as I stepped out on to the windy platform overhanging Seascale beach, I had no inkling how much my further Cumbrian experience was going to contribute to my writing, or how deeply my feeling for the region would develop.

The headmaster came forward to greet me. 'Mac' was fractionally younger than myself, neatly moustached with saturnine good looks, civil but crisp in manner. He looked tough, and I later found him a vigorous games-player, though I believe some medical reason disqualified him for military service. He was reserved to the point of remoteness, though a dry humour occasionally flashed out in terse syllables. He was unmarried.

As we shook hands we were joined by another new master, my fellow-traveller, had we but identified each other, for some hours past. Betham was still younger, with powerfully lensed spectacles. He and I, Mac explained as he drove us inland, would share a cottage across the yard from the house, though we should take all our meals in the dining-hall.

This cottage proved to be a pleasant old building, smartly whitewashed in Cumbrian style with glossy black window-frames, facing the road across a tiny apron of grass. Beyond, the riding-field curved to the sunset sky, with the school's eight ponies munching contentedly.

On the ground floor, besides a music-room and a classroom whose few desks promised manageable groups, there was the sitting-room Betham and I were to share. It was shabby but comfortable enough, with a writing-table each, an electric fire and an electric kettle. Upstairs, the bathroom had encouragingly hot water. Besides our own bedrooms there were one or two others, obviously unused, which I privately noted as potential married quarters. Betham was a bachelor, so there would be no competition. It was a little premature, though, to start scheming.

We had been told to arrive a day before the boys, so there was a quiet interval for the registering of first impressions. They were good. The sheer beauty of the place was arresting. Whether at meals in the dining-room, or standing at the black-board in the classrooms of the main building, we had Wasdale Screes dramatically framed in the tall windows. From the tennis-lawn outside, or the games field that lay beyond a little wood-land, we had a wider panorama, swinging leftwards to take in Scafell Pike, Great Gable, and the high wastes of Copeland Forest.

I had come, all unknowingly, to Bannerdale, about which, in the years to come, I was going to write *No Boats on Bannermere* and its four sequels.

Bannermere will not be found on any map. There is a Banner

Dale, scarcely more than a mile long, just east of Saddleback, and Bannerdale Crags looking down upon it, but I have never seen them. My own Bannerdale, with its lake and forbidden islet and its sombre mountain Black Banner lowering over it, is one of those private fantasy regions that authors, and especially children's authors, love to create. It is a pastiche, three parts Wasdale, one part Eskdale, with bits and pieces from elsewhere. The 'Gates of Bannerdale' were taken from the Jaws of Borrowdale, 'Black Banner' was suggested by the real mountain, Black Sail, and my little town of 'Winthwaite' is Cockermouth, shifted southwards for literary convenience. It was not till seven or eight years later that, recollecting a good deal of emotion in a certain amount of tranquillity, I began to invent this little world. Nowadays I can perhaps say, without blatant immodesty, that it does not 'exist merely in my own mind' but exists also in the minds of a lot of people who, in childhood or later, have read the stories I laid there. Not only British children, but – oddly and gratifyingly – Japanese, Swedes, Brazilians and others equally remote.

All this lay far in the future. My immediate preoccupation was my new job and my survival in it after half-term, when either side would be free to give notice.

I was a trifle shaken when my employer remarked that he had noticed, ten days earlier, the *Sunday Times* review of my second novel, *Only Natural*. It is a general rule of life that an author's friends miss any good reviews he gets. They see only, and never fail to tell him about, the wounding ones. In this case Ralph Straus had been flattering enough, but I could have wished that his summary of my plot had escaped the headmaster's eye. The 'only natural' behaviour of my hero and heroine, commonplace today, was not universally acceptable in 1940 – and they were both members of the teaching profession.

True, judging from hints picked up, I guessed that Mac was not the sole proprietor of the school. There appeared to be a senior partner, a certain Major, who had gone back into khaki. But Mac was headmaster and in complete control, and he was not a young man whose views on life, and sex in particular, were easy to divine.

It was a tiny, enclosed world I had entered. I had to adjust myself to a new atmosphere and vocabulary. A note was a chit, a satisfactory occurrence was a good show. I saw most, of course, of Betham, whose family connections, I believe, were military and Indian. The teaching staff was completed by the governess for the smallest boys, a tall, dark and handsome young woman, product of a southern cathedral close. She taught music, also, and riding. She lived in the main building, when not actually in the saddle, mucking out or cleaning tack, and as there was no true common room we saw little of her except at meals. It was then, too, that we met the elderly, agreeable housekeeper and the young matron. We were served by immaculately capped-and-aproned maids, with whom one never exchanged more than a correct word and an impersonal smile. The food, by wartime standards, was very good.

And the boys? I found them likeable, and my slight fore-bodings about lessons, discipline – and above all games – were soon forgotten.

There were only nineteen at first, increasing later to about thirty as fears of invasion made Cumberland attractive. We had one or two amiable blockheads, but mainly they were intelligent and the school did allow them to develop as individuals. A boy I quickly noticed was the cheerfully grinning little Philip Huggins, nephew of Rhodesia's first prime minister, one of those rare rewarding pupils who are as alert over a book as they are behind the scrum. Years later, having taken his degree, he came out to visit me at Abingdon. He was just leaving with a Himalayan expedition, on which he died, a tragic waste, a few months afterwards. Another, with a keen love of nature and better luck in his subsequent explorations, was Nigel Hepper, who became an authority on African flora at Kew. Tam Dalyell, the future Labour M.P., entered the school some terms later. We must be sure to call him 'Dalyell of the Binns', Mac warned us. His mother was immensely proud of his descent from the seventeenth-century Tam, the soldier-of-fortune who had served the Muscovite Tsar and founded the Scots Greys.

Teaching boys of this quality in small groups was a congenial task. The subjects were somewhat eccentrically distributed among the staff. Mac, who had read English at Oxford, took the Latin. I, whose highest academic attainment was my open

Classics scholarship, taught no Latin but was in charge of English, History and Geography, though I had given up the two latter subjects before I was thirteen. Betham, with a Cambridge History degree and an obsession about Cardinal Wolsey – I wonder if he has *yet* written his promised book on that statesman – was responsible for all the French except that imparted to the smallest boys. They learned theirs from the riding-mistress, who one night at dinner frankly admitted her linguistic limitations, so frankly indeed that I was able to inquire, without offence, 'What happens if they ask for a French word you don't know?'

'I invent it,' she confessed blithely, Mac's attention being engaged elsewhere.

'Couldn't that be awkward later on?'

'Oh, no, Trease. They never *remember* anything.'

In fact, the school had good Common Entrance and scholarship results. At the under-fourteen stage there was probably something to be said for our not teaching the subjects we knew most about. It narrowed the gulf between master and pupil. It was also perhaps as well that I was not expected to take the riding. With my own group of subjects I was very happy, teaching them in close relation. Small as the classes were, the boys produced a mass of work to be corrected. When we reached the 1914 war their curiosity was insatiable. They wrote unbidden, till my red ink failed and I begged for respite. It was partly the recollection of those enthusiastic twelve-year-olds, with their passionate interest in recent history and their too often underrated powers of comprehension, that fortified my confidence when, long afterwards, I conceived the idea of setting out the whole chronicle in *This Is Your Century*.

During my early weeks at Gosforth, however, I was fully occupied with the Normans and Saxons. Outside school hours, it was the Second World War, not the first, that filled my mind.

That war was now beginning in earnest. Hitler's surprise attacks on Norway and Denmark had taken place just before my arrival in Cumberland. I had been there scarcely ten days when he launched his full-scale blitzkrieg on the Low Countries. The next month or two I recall as a period of unbroken sunshine and, so far as the news was concerned, unremitting gloom.

Betham and I used to sit in the cottage on those summer evenings, listening to the radio bulletins. As a colonel's son, he
was inclined to pontificate on strategy.

The worst disasters, Dunkirk and the French capitulation,
did not come until after half-term, itself an anxiously awaited
date in my private calendar. Mac had made no comment on
my teaching and I had met with no problems of discipline, but,
though I took my turn with the games supervision, I could make
no useful contribution as a coach, and I must have been a
disappointment when he wanted a fourth for tennis on Sunday
afternoons.

Half-term came, but no termination of my contract. I was
relieved, but there was a moment when I was wildly tempted
to give notice myself. Despite petrol rationing a good crowd
of parents had turned up and tea was set out in the dining-hall,
where normally Betham and I joined the matron, housekeeper
and riding-mistress for this welcome interlude between games
and lessons. That day it was made clear to us that our presence
was not desired. A maid would bring us a tray in the cottage.
Only once or twice in all my time there was I ever introduced –
unavoidably – to the parents of the boys I taught. We felt like
tutors in an eighteenth-century noble household, abruptly rele-
gated to the servants' hall.

I had been making plans for Marian and Jocelyn to come up
for a few days in the latter part of the term. I had considered a
discreet inquiry about the empty, but fully furnished, guest-room
adjoining my own. I realised now that it would be unwise.
Instead, I found accommodation at the farmhouse next door, and
in July we were able to spend a few nights together there. At
the school itself, however, there was no welcome. There was
a short, awkward conversation on the playing-field when I made
the introductions, but no more. To the best of my recollection
(and that recollection is clearly etched in the corrosive of bottled-
up emotion) Marian was never invited into the main building,
much less offered a cup of tea. Why? God knows. I suppose,
on reflection, that marriage was not recognised in that establishment, except for the parents who had to produce pupils. Nobody
else, male or female, was married. I must have seemed an in-
convenient freak.

How trivial it all seems now! But of such bygone trivia is
social history made.

We had by this time far weightier worries to contend with.
Two months had transformed the war situation, and with it the
existence, tranquil at least, however dull and lonely, to which I
had left Marian at Abingdon.

Now Britain faced invasion. Many children were being sent
abroad for safety. Unlike my own relatives, all concentrated in
Nottingham, Marian's were excessively scattered, her father in
Manitoba, her brother in Nevada, her sister in Sydney. She was
bombarded with kindly offers, begging her at least to send
Jocelyn across the Atlantic or to Australia. The unshared responsibility of deciding was too much. This was something we
had to talk out together. I remember a wretched off-duty afternoon when we lay on the beach at Seascale while the object of
our discussion pottered happily amid the sand.

Marian spared me at the time the knowledge of another
development that had added to the strain. The current fear of
invasion was accompanied by something like the spy-mania
which gripped people in 1914. The talk was now of Fifth
Columns and Nazi parachutists in exotic disguises. At Radley a
gentle Austrian refugee we knew, himself a fugitive from Hitler,
was sent to a detention-camp in the Isle of Man. Although all
my personal friends had known for weeks beforehand that I was
taking a post in Cumberland, my disappearance started the most
sinister rumours. It is not pleasant to live on a very small hous-
ing estate where the neighbouring housewives believe that your
husband has been secretly whisked off to prison as an enemy
agent – Nazi or Russian, what was the difference? – and where
you have absolutely no chance to scotch the story and convince
them that in fact, blissfully unaware of their innuendoes, he is
teaching the sons of country gentlemen the glorious history of
the Island Race. It seems ludicrous now. For Marian it was not
so funny. By the time she came up to Gosforth she was feeling
these combined stresses acutely.

During those anxious days together we agreed on a com-
promise. She and Jocelyn would stay in England and take their
chance with the vast majority, but they would accept my mother's
invitation to join her in Nottingham, which, though an industrial

city, might be safer than the Thames valley. Mother, now
elderly and alone, would thus be less likely to have strangers
billeted on her.

There seemed no hope of arranging anything in Gosforth.
The farm had no permanent accommodation, my other local
inquiries drew blank, and obviously the school was going to do
nothing. In any case, how long should I be there? Dunkirk had
touched off a new series of appeals and proclamations. Again,
men with possible qualifications as officers were asked to send
in their names, so I submitted mine for the second time.

Marian went home to Abingdon, tidied up the house and let
it furnished to an Eastbourne College master who had been
evacuated to Radley. When term ended I joined Marian and
Jocelyn at the old home in Portland Road, where my earliest
coherent memories had begun. The cellars in which I had once
sheltered from the Kaiser's zeppelins were once more ready
with blankets and candles. The Luftwaffe had by now started
on London.

During those holidays I was called for interview at Lincoln
Barracks. It was an old-fashioned, gentlemanly affair. I was
asked about family connections with the Army and personal
preferences. Having no technical qualifications I could not
imagine myself in anything but the humble infantry, so for this
I was duly accepted and told to wait until called.

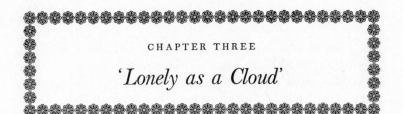

CHAPTER THREE

'Lonely as a Cloud'

S EPTEMBER found me back in Cumberland, waiting as in the September of the previous year.

> But the waiting time, my brothers,
> Is the hardest time of all,

wrote Sarah Doudney, an American poet otherwise unfamiliar to me. Who would contradict her?

Gosforth was strangely detached from the war, though, by an odd chance, I was never nearer to a bomb than when a mine, intended for the Solway Firth, rattled our windows one night and gouged an immense crater in the adjacent fields.

One lunch-hour in November a panting maid tracked me down. My wife was on the line. We did not normally telephone – it was all too difficult – so I rushed off in alarm.

Marian, a thin voice far away, said: 'I just wanted to let you know we're all right.'

'All right?'

'It wasn't us. The "midland city" wasn't Nottingham.'

I had heard no radio news that morning. I had missed the B.B.C. announcement of a devastating air raid on 'a midland city'. Places were not named in those days for fear of helping the enemy, and Marian's immediate thought had been to reassure me. Subsequent bulletins disclosed that the bombed city was Coventry. Such a raid, opening a new and more ferocious phase of the war, could not be hushed up. Truth was safer than proliferating rumour.

Nottingham never became a major target. Its worst raid was when the German bombers attacked it in error, mistaking it for the engineering town of Derby. Marian and Jocelyn were luckily away, visiting Marian's aunt at Wisbech. There were other, nerve-racking nights in the cellar, with bombs crashing in the distance, but none too near. Jocelyn had only a dim notion of what was happening. Marian explained that the noises were made by the naughty soldiers billeted further up the street. Tomorrow, their sergeant-major would punish them.

The term passed without any summons from the War Office. By this time the selection for commissions was becoming much more stringent, and future officers were having to pass first through the ranks. Eventually I was called for my medical examination with the rest of my age-group in the ordinary way, but I was still waiting when we came to the third September of the war.

It was a period one still aches to remember. There was nothing remarkable in our prosaic experience. We were just one young family, out of millions in a similar or worse situation, whose normal life together had been abruptly turned off, as though by a malign valve.

Marian had the worst of it. She did not complain then, and would not thank me now for trying to depict at second hand the lot of a young mother with a child, transplanted to a little-known city made drab and grim by black-out and restrictions. My own mother preferred to run the house herself. Once Jocelyn was installed at a little private school close by, Marian did some teaching and gave a few talks to women in the Army. She made one or two good friends and she attended some of the exceptionally good evening classes that were available, and enthusiastically supported, in those war-time winters. But I knew how homesick she often was, and we discussed the possibility of her return to Abingdon. 'If the war turns definitely in our favour,' I wrote, 'with no risk of invasion.' But I added that it looked 'like being a long struggle, lasting into 1943, 44 or 45'.

I wrote that in autumn, 1941. Russia, but not Japan, was now in the fight.

Jocelyn was just five. Increasingly I grudged the months of term when we were kept apart, though the holidays together in Nottingham kept us from becoming strangers. I remember arriving late one night. She woke when I peeped into her room, blinked, sat up, surveyed me with a bleary but welcoming smile, and remarked with immense deliberation, 'Hullo, Daddy! I will see *more* of you in the morning.' She then closed her eyes dis-missively, relapsed on to the pillow, and was gone.

Her own term continued another day or two, so that I was in time for the concert. Being one of the youngest, she performed early in the programme. She had to recite 'Christopher Robin is saying his prayers', and I listened with mingled nausea and paternal pride. After each item, the performer came down off the stage and took a seat in the front rows left vacant for the purpose. At this point Jocelyn saw Marian and myself sitting halfway down the hall and gave us a wave of recognition, unfor-tunately adding, in those clear tones that had already been favourably commented upon as carrying to the very back of the audience: 'Hullo, Mummy! Hullo, Daddy! *Are* you staying to the bitter end?'

She still seemed to regard my presence in the house as normal, my absence in Cumberland as abnormal, not the other way round. That was something to be thankful for.

As to the effects of separation on myself I tried to be philo-sophical. As a writer I knew the dividend that can be drawn from solitude, but in Cumberland I had far more solitude than I liked. I knew loneliness as I had never known it since meeting Marian. Betham left for a job at Bradfield and for one term I was quite alone in the cottage, since his work was taken over by a girl. Then she in turn left to join the Women's Royal Naval Service, and two masters arrived, one fresh from school himself, the other very deaf, both agreeable enough, but neither sharing deeply in my own interests and concerns. I wrote impatiently to Marian:

The weather is horrible, but this afternoon I took Roger again and Philip Huggins up Wasdale. We did about 5 miles over soaking moors, had a delicious scrambled-egg tea, and did another 5 m. home along the road in the dusk. They're very nice boys, and certainly the best company available. Of course, they really live in a world apart, like another species, but a certain amount of tacit, unsentimental affection can pass between us. I should rate them as midway between humans and spaniels. We *have* no humans or spaniels.

Those walks, sometimes with a few boys, more often alone . . .
that countryside, so sublime, but in my loneliness so poignant.
. . . Yeats wrote, in a different context, 'A terrible beauty
is born', and to me in some moods Wasdale's beauty was
indeed terrible. The ghost of those desolate days was partly
exorcised when I came to write Bannermere stories, but not
entirely.

My favourite walk lay up a dale so unfrequented that I thought
of it romantically as my secret valley. The Bleng, a busy, frothy
little river, scarcely named in guide-books, emerged to public
gaze near an old watermill outside the village and ran off, un-
regarded, among the fields. But upstream a rough track led to
a gate and thence to a high plank-bridge and a steep, tree-hung,
boulder-strewn ravine.

I discovered Blengdale in my first week and thereafter
explored it in all seasons. I knew it in midsummer, when a dozen
natural bathing-pools lay blue beneath the sandy red cliffs and
the shaggy plantations of conifer. I knew it in spring and autumn,
and when yard-long icicles dangled like swords from the over-
hangs, when the swollen river raced blackly round snow-crusted
rocks, and when impassable drifts blocked off the upper valley.
In all those walks, except for any boys I took, I only once saw
other people, two men laying a hound-trail.

There was infinite variety. I could follow the right bank or
the left, clatter over loose stones at the water's edge, take the
airy high-level route between the young trees, or the dark
tunnel hacked through the full-grown woodland, or the grass
ribbon curling through the bracken. Sometimes near, sometimes
a hundred feet below, the river came bouncing down in a sequence
of rapids. It was the Canadian backwoods in miniature, and the
boys loved it, imagining Indian ambushes at every turn. There
was a second foot-bridge, a perilous trifle of slats and wires
festooned across the boiling water. We had to dash across this
at full pelt, my companions insisting that it was swept by enemy
fire.

Where the woods ended there was sombre desolation, but
with superb heights swimming into view beyond, Seatallan
with its sharp northward face, unmistakable, High Fell and
Haycock soaring above Gower Crag, and the dark rampart of

Brown Band. They stood round like an amphitheatre. Somewhere in the boggy floor at their feet the river was born.

I was content to stop short of that ultimate morass. Here, at a spot marked on the map as Sergeant's Ford, was the only path which crossed my valley at right-angles, probably an old smugglers' route into Wasdale from the coast near Calderbridge. Here too, on a rounded hillside mystifyingly dubbed Sampson's Bratfull, Gothic type promised 'cairns' and 'tumuli'. The boys poked round with their knives, hoping for skeletons.

On the day I best remember I was alone. The December examinations had given me the whole day off. The morning was pure Swiss postcard, the snow on the higher fells rose-pink in the sunrise, the shadows really blue. On a shelf beside a pool I found a freshly killed salmon, one neat otter-bite through its back. It was almost three feet, measured against my walking-stick, and I was never forgiven for not hurrying back to school with it. An hour later, among the cairns, I saw a mountain fox, proud in his snow-white winter waistcoat, his tawny side-view unchanged. I crouched behind the stones as he loped across the fell. He was uneasy; he had an idea I was there. From time to time he paused, wheeled to face me, and vanished like a snuffed-out flame. Then, reassured, he would turn and go on again, red against the dazzling crystals, printing a dotted line. That was the last time I saw the head of my valley.

Such moments went into my notebook. Simple and unsensational, they are sufficient raw material for the writer, even the writer of adventure stories. He does not need to have had adventures. If he can gather seeds, however tiny, from reality, his imagination will grow them to sizes, shapes and colours as required.

Also into my notebook went scraps of dialogue, character-sketches, authentic local scenes – a farmer's wife at Wasdale, a solitary wood-carver in Eskdale, the bustle of a farmyard auction. Some of the material was later to go straight into the Bannermere stories. Other bits would be transmuted and transferred to other centuries and other countries. Characters I have never taken entire from life, and, if I have used any particularly recognisable mannerism, I have felt safer if the story was set in some remote period. Thus, in *Word to Caesar*, the voluble matron with the recurrent trick of demanding, 'But *why?*' had a twentieth-century model. But so, for that matter, did the opinionated Oxford undergraduate in *The Gates of Bannerdale* whose automatic reaction was to cry, 'Oh, I don't agree!' and, though the original read the book, he never complained. No doubt my characterisation would have been stronger if I had been bolder, like D.H. Lawrence or Nancy Mitford, and lifted entire figures unaltered from my own life. Perhaps the nearest I came to it was in Kingsford, the headmaster in the Bannermere stories, modelled on the craggy, alarming but lovable history-master, R. S. Bridge, who had loomed so large in my own schooldays. There is something of Bridge, too, in Doctor Pharaoh, the Cromwellian headmaster in *The Grey Adventurer* and *Silver Guard*. His interesting and evocative surname I took from the lintel of an inn near Gosforth, where it was the name of the licensee.

An odd business, this magpie accumulation of material. If one dates each entry, one gets many a surprise in later years, discovering how far back a particular book can be traced and in what forgotten circumstances the initial idea was conceived.

There was, for instance, the October day when I cycled over into Eskdale and walked up to the Roman camp at Hardknott, which Marian and I had visited in happier days. Hardknott was to provide, fourteen years later, the British setting for the first chapter of *Word to Caesar*. When I planned the book, I was anxious to get away from the national bias which, in so many stories of that epoch, seems to suggest that the Romans are interesting only as the invaders of Britain. I wanted to tell children about the Romans in Italy, the Romans of the Silver Age of classical literature (I worked in an exiled poet, another Ovid with altered dates) and above all the Romans of a peaceful, efficiently united Europe, the empire of Hadrian. But in dealing with an apparently remote period and setting one must establish a bridge, so I felt it best to open the tale with Hardknott and Ravenglass in Britain, and then set the plot moving that would carry my hero to Arles, Ostia, Rome and the Bay of Naples.

That autumn afternoon, however, I walked the overgrown ramparts and sought for traces of the bath-house without a notion of the use I should one day make of them, the bath-house

in particular, indispensable to my hero's escape when the tribes-
men overrun the camp at the opening of the story. In fact, as
my notebook reminds me, I was fresh from a history class and
could not clear my mind of the Civil War.

I was thinking of a possible story, which I wrote six years
later, entitled *Silver Guard* and set partly in Cumberland. I had
been explaining to the boys that, if we could have polled a
representative ten Englishmen in 1642, we might have found
one Cavalier, one Roundhead, and eight just praying for the
whole thing to stop and let them get on with their own lives.
This view cut right across my pupils' prejudices. It was then
virtually obligatory to show the Cavaliers as heroes. I thought
it would be a good idea to write a story presenting a more
objective picture from the angle of a New England colonist,
returning to Oxford to study just when the university was
disrupted by the unwelcome war.

I was already moving away from the crude partisan stand-
point of my earliest stories, *Bows Against the Barons* and *Comrades for the Charter*. In 1940, just before I went to Cumberland,
George Orwell had reviewed my new novel, *Only Natural*, in
Tribune:

> If I say that I have 'discovered' Mr Geoffrey Trease, I shall
> be told rightly enough that I ought to have discovered him
> long ago, but the fact is that I had never heard his name
> until a couple of months back. He is that creature we have
> long been needing, a 'light' Left-wing writer, rebellious but
> human, a sort of P. G. Wodehouse after a course of Marx. . . .
> You know you are in for a good laugh, and you get it. Don't
> miss this book.

Encouraged by these kind words, I had written to Orwell.
If he was so concerned about the reactionary nature of children's
literature – he had just fired his famous broadside on that subject
in *Inside the Whale* – it was galling for me that he should be so
ignorant of what I had been trying to do in that field for the
previous six years. I suggested that with his reputation and
influence something more might be done. He answered warmly,
if a little wryly, demolishing my assumption that he was famous
and established. His books, he told me frankly, sold between

one and two thousand copies. But he was interested in what I said, and in fact several people had now drawn his attention to my children's books. He thought the time might be ripe for some Leftish juvenile publishing scheme, pink in shade, perhaps backed by the T.U.C. or the Liberal *News Chronicle*. Not having read *Homage to Catalonia*, and being unaware of his disenchantment with the official Communist line, I did not fully appreciate his quip that, if Lawrence & Wishart did it, they would want books like 'Boys of the Ogpu' or 'The Young Liquidators'. They were my original publishers and I had nothing against them, but I realised later why Orwell could not have worked with them. In any case, nothing came of our discussions. They were overtaken by events – Dunkirk and the fall of France – and the idea lapsed.

My own reforming zeal, however, was undiminished. Through Desmond Hawkins, whom I had known in my Bloomsbury days, I obtained an introduction to T. C. Worsley of the *New Statesman*. Desmond thought I 'obviously had the best claim to the job' of reviewing 'boys' books', as we still called them in 1940. Worsley sent me a batch and I wrote a rather fierce article entitled 'Niggers, Kings and Queens'.

When is the main body of juvenile fiction going to make a perceptible move forward? . . . Our world may be in ferment but our annual accumulation of juveniles still depict, in vigorous line-drawing and exclamatory narrative, the good old world of the open spaces. Here, for our Christmas comfort, is an Africa which knows not Mussolini, and in which the beneficent rule of the Englishman cannot conceivably be disturbed by anything less than a fanciful revolt of natives; a Frontier which ignores the problems of the sub-continent pressing upon it from behind; and a bygone world-which-never-was of cavaliers talking like Sir John Martin-Harvey. . . . While our school-teachers struggle manfully to prepare children for the world of – shall we say 1945? – the story-books condition them for a certain limited but comfortable corner some forty years before.

Worsley pronounced my review 'admirable' and sent me

further parcels at intervals, though juvenile publishing was more seasonal than it is now and there was not much work for me outside the pre-Christmas period. Still, it was the first time that a well-known paper had given me a chance to ventilate the unorthodox views I was later to develop in *Tales Out of School*. Most of the new children's books were so bad then that it was easy, and not unjustifiable, to poke fun at them in the style most acceptable to the *New Statesman* public. The experience of this reviewing, plus observation of the books the boys were reading, caused me to broaden the front of my attack. False history, though it continued to infuriate me, was not the only enemy. And I was realising too – perhaps Orwell's quip had helped? – that false history from the Right should not be countered with false history from the Left. And the very process of trying to teach boys honestly was giving me a new reverence for objective truth.

Criticism apart, there was so much I wanted to write myself, if only I survived the war. In other notebook entries for 1940 and 1941 I can detect the seeds that grew into *Trumpets in the West* (1947), the brief but significant appearance of Erasmus in *The Hills of Varna* (1948), and the title at least of my adult novel, *Snared Nightingale*, which surfaces in the notebook again in 1949 but was not written until 1955. An elephant's pregnancy cannot compete in duration with an author's, but with the author the development of the embryo may not be so continuous a process, save in his subconscious.

Though I note the idea for a book the moment it occurs to me – a theme, a character, a situation – I prefer not to think about it in detail until I know I am free to start work in earnest. Otherwise, the inspiration goes cold, much as it does if you talk about it too soon to other people. Only when I am ready to go into production, which may be years later, do I begin the special reading and research, the shuffling of the bits of paper with random notes on the characters and incidents. At this point the research and the invention proceed side by side, reacting on each other. Something originally imagined must be checked, justified, made plausible and three-dimensional, by thumbing through the reference books. Conversely, that research may produce fresh or improved ideas for the fiction. Some dry fact from social history may suggest a dramatic incident or a quirk of human character that will fit splendidly into the plan. I say 'plan' because, as the written notes multiply, it becomes possible to shape them into a coherent sequence. I have never been one of those talented, confident writers who can start with a character or a situation and (they claim) let the book develop from there as it will.

As a boy, writing a three-act play with William Archer's *Play-making* at my elbow, I accepted the architectural conception and applied it afterwards to books as well. I had to know my final curtain in advance and plan to lead up to it from the first raising of that curtain (in those good old days when there *was* a curtain to enhance the magic) at the beginning of the entertainment. Exits and entrances had to be planned, clues planted ready for the dénouement, characters portrayed so that their necessary subsequent behaviour should seem inevitable. And so with a novel, whether for children or for adults. Often I work with a set of blank slips or filing-cards, one for each chapter. The first – that is to say, the last – can be quickly completed, with a jotted summary of the final scene. If, as commonly happens, I have thought of my opening, it is easy to complete a second slip and label it 'Chapter 1'. Perhaps fourteen blank slips remain, but there should at this stage be ample to fill them. The second chapter, or the penultimate, may be obvious. It is harder, for a moment, to say that a particular episode will provide Chapter 7 or Chapter 9. But by degrees the slips are filled in, even though some remain unnumbered, and they are shuffled about on the table until, with luck, an order is achieved in which each chapter follows naturally from the one before, and this sequence can be typed out as a single-sheet synopsis.

This procedure is not always necessary, and it is never rigid. Where the story closely follows actual historical events, such as the French Revolution, the Russian, or the campaigns of Garibaldi, it is unnecessary because the events impose their own sequence, but with an invented plot like that of *Popinjay Stairs* or *Word to Caesar* it can be very helpful. In the case of *Popinjay Stairs*, which was to be first a four-part radio-play and then a book, there had to be two designs. The usual slips of paper were shuffled to get the sequence of chapters (which finally came to

eighteen) but I also took a large sheet, quartered it, and made
sure that, with four or five of the future prose chapters assigned
to each quarter, one of the major dramatic moments would
come pat, as a 'cliff-hanger', at the end of each weekly instalment.

That was in 1973. But my general writing methods – and
certainly my plot-construction – were substantially the same
thirty years earlier. They may sound repellently contrived to
those with a highfalutin conception of the way in which an
artist creates. The truth is otherwise. Such procedures – flexible,
rule-of-thumb – are not inimical to inspiration and integrity;
they are humble, helpful accessories in the fulfilment of his
deeper purpose. 'Contrivance' belongs to the story which has
not been adequately planned, and which therefore requires coin-
cidences and other unconvincing subterfuges to bring it to some
kind of solution.

Without some kind of system, I could not have written much
at Gosforth. A schoolmaster cannot afford to lose all sense of
time and follow where inspiration leads him – and pure inspiration does not take kindly to enforced breaks for lessons, games
and supervision duties. It is reassuring, when returning to the
unfinished paragraph, to see a written synopsis beside the typewriter, especially when a colleague is snorting over the newspaper in the same small room.

Those were the circumstances in which I wrote my next book
for Basil Blackwell. I called it *The Grey Adventurer*. My hero
was the orphan of a Cromwellian colonel during the Restoration
reprisals. The title expressed not only my unfashionable sympathy with the drab-suited supporters of Parliament but also
my desire to treat those themes commonly ignored as dull and
'unromantic'.

Encouraged by the enthusiasm of Vanguard Press for *Cue for
Treason*, I tried to increase the transatlantic appeal of this new
story by dispatching my hero to the then freshly founded colony
of North Carolina. It was a naïve mistake, for I had never myself
set foot in America. Such deliberate 'catering' is in any case
most unwise. Good books are not produced by conscious market-
study. Contact with children, which insensibly affects one's
manner of story-telling, may be helpful in a general, and rather

minor, way, but some authors have managed quite well without it.

I used to read *The Grey Adventurer* to the boys on wet afternoons, chapter by chapter as it was written. Reading aloud
exposed any obscurities, longueurs, awkward phrasings, and
unintentional – sometimes hilarious – ambiguities. Even today,
looking over a typescript, I can fancy myself back in that school-
room with the intent, grey-jerseyed cluster, the rain slashing
the glass, the dirty mist blotting out the fells. My phantom
audience can still sometimes save me from disaster.

Over twenty years later, in *Follow My Black Plume* (Garibaldi's defence of Rome in 1849), I wanted to engage some of
my readers' sympathy for his less glamorous colleague, Mazzini.
Mazzini's modesty, I was sure, would appeal to them. One of
my historical sources mentioned that the patriot leader, installed
in the uncongenial splendours of the Quirinal, 'hunted for a room
small enough to feel at home in'. In my first draft I unguardedly
allowed my impressionable young heroine to exclaim: 'He is
the most important man here and he is using the smallest room
in the palace as his office.' As soon as I reread this I heard, in
imagination, a great hoot of delight go up from my invisible
listeners. I hastily rephrased the sentence, and then, realising
also how likely many young readers would be to mispronounce
'Quirinal', I worked back over the whole passage and cut out
all but one indispensable mention of the name.

In such ways as these, and of course in more general and
more important respects – the maintenance of awareness about
young people's tastes, interests and prejudices – such contact is
valuable, but it should not develop into a deliberate consumer-
research that determines both the content of the story and its
packaging. The boys' previous responses might unconsciously
affect me, but I never put things in, or left them out, at variance
with my plan. I still wrote what I wanted to write. The boys'
response reassured me that I was on course. I never charted
that course to please them, let alone altered it.

In another, special sense I got something from those wet
afternoons. They offset, in advance, what might in later years
have become an unconscious orientation towards girl readers,
when each chapter was read, fresh from the typewriter, to
Jocelyn on her return from school. It is difficult not to be in-

fluenced, however insensibly, by a particular and constant author-listener relationship like that.

Fortunately girls have always seemed to me more tolerant than boys – in this context, at least. They will often accept a boy-centred story whereas one told from the heroine's point of view faces a barrier of young male prejudice. With *Cue for Treason* I had broken away completely from the conventional pre-war classification of 'books for boys' and 'books for girls', as though they were school lavatories. I wanted my stories to appeal equally to both sexes. To achieve this, I learned, they still needed to retain a certain masculine bias, not enough to repel the girls, but one which I expressed to myself, in a crude rule-of-thumb manner, as a sixty–forty percentage. Occasionally, wanting to tell the story from more than one point of view, I have alternated chapters centred on the hero and the heroine respectively. But, though Chapter 2 might be especially 'hers', I never dared make Chapter 1 anything but 'his'. I could picture too many youthful male chauvinists tossing the book aside after a disgusted glance at the opening pages.

To a male writer such bias came, alas, by nature. But having a daughter, and no son, as family audience might in after-time have over-influenced my style of story-telling, so I still feel in debt to those boys in Cumberland long ago.

I finished *The Grey Adventurer* in June 1941. But in that same year I had written something quite different, of which the boys knew nothing. The theatres had been allowed to reopen only a few weeks after the outbreak of war, and though my controversial *Colony* had no hope of resurrection I was ready to have another go at the West End.

CHAPTER FOUR

Dramatic Interludes

M Y affair with the theatre was of long standing. I say 'affair' because, long and strong though it was, it never became the single-minded devotion which is generally vital to success. Galsworthy and Maugham were exceptional. They were equally eminent as novelists. But Shaw had to stop trying to write novels before he broke into the theatre, whereas Lawrence, whose potential as a playwright was recognised only long after his death, was never able, what with illness, absence abroad, and an unaccommodating temperament, to thrust open a door that was at least ajar. The would-be dramatist needs a streak of monomania, a conviction that the theatre, and only the theatre, will satisfy his need. Only this will carry him through the frustrations of that crazy, unjust, illogical world. If he writes adequately enough to be published in other literary forms, it merely blunts his determination.

My own affair, as I now see it to have been, was rooted in childhood, when I first saw the magic flush of the footlights suffuse the curtain and heard the crash and blare of the overture. My brother Bill made me a toy theatre. I cast my plays with those cut-out sheets of 'penny plain, twopence coloured' from a little shop, called the Doll's House, at the top of the street. Or, being fond of drawing and painting, I made my own paper characters and scenery. The toy outgrown, I went on to compose plays I could act with my friends. Later still, there was the school dramatic society. Mostly that meant playing in classics – I was the tiresome Claudio in *Much Ado* (was that a bit of crafty type-casting?) and Sir Lucius O'Trigger and Marlowe's Doctor Faustus. But I had my hour, or rather two evenings, of glory as an embryo dramatist, when at seventeen I directed my own play.

Throughout my schooldays, I had been an addicted theatre-goer. My tastes (and, sometimes I almost feared, my anatomy) were shaped in the execrably uncomfortable gallery of the Nottingham Theatre Royal, from whose remote height I peered down upon the best touring companies of the 1920s. A few still made a nightly change of programme, so that – to Hell with homework! – I could enjoy several plays by Shakespeare or Shaw between Monday and Saturday. One unforgettable Friday I was in my seat by half-past five, when Esmé Percy and the Macdona Players began a marathon one-night-only performance of *Man and Superman* in its entirety. This was 'theatre' as I knew it – queues in the rain, the lung-bursting clatter up the concrete steps, titled actor-managers, *Sir* Frank Benson, *Sir* John Martin-Harvey, gracious curtain-speeches like papal bene-dictions, romance, melodrama, deathly hushes, rolls of cosmic laughter round the plushy auditorium . . . strong meat, but nourishing.

London in the early 1930s did little to change the picture. The young Gielgud was at the Old Vic. The West End was a galaxy of stars, Cedric Hardwicke, Fay Compton, Gwen Frang-con-Davies and many more. I was a year or two older, a thought more sophisticated and critical, but the essential glamour was undimmed. I saw the theatre as a place of polish and panache, in which the successful writer enjoyed the best of both worlds, flaying social evils in the tradition of Ibsen, Shaw and Gals-worthy, yet taking his bow, well tailored and imperturbable, to ecstatic cries of 'Author!' from the well-dined stalls. Gilt and cherub chandeliers, sweeping staircases and rustling ladies and foyers bubbling with ecstatic praise made up the enchanted world you swam through if you could write plays.

The alluring fantasy that I should one day be part of it was pushed into the background by other pressures in my first years as a writer, but in 1939 it suddenly seemed capable of realisation. Two years earlier I had been drawn back almost accidentally into dramatic writing. A one-act comedy, *After the Tempest*, a satirical glimpse into the future, twenty years after a catastro-phic world war, had been originally dashed off for a club evening of the Abingdon amateurs. They had liked it enough to make it their entry for the Welwyn Drama Festival, where Miles

Malleson had judged it best of more than twenty productions
and also given it the new-play prize against six competitors.
An excerpt had been shown on television and J. W. Marriott
had chosen it for his *Best One-act Plays of 1938.*

This had encouraged me to write a longer, more serious play
and offer it to Unity Theatre, a left-wing club theatre then
operating near King's Cross with the powerful backing of many
well-known theatrical and public figures. It was independent of
the censor, it was open six nights a week, including Sundays,
and its standards earned it full press coverage. It possessed a
brilliant director in Herbert Marshall, a self-educated Londoner
who had acquired his theatrical expertise by battling his way
through the most rigorous training in Moscow. Today, dynamic
and irrepressible as ever, he is a professor at the superbly
equipped centre for the performing arts at Southern Illinois
University.

To *Colony* Bert brought all his own talents, developed in the
Stanislavsky tradition. The play was set on an imaginary tropical
island. It was an attack on imperialism in general, but it had
special contemporary relevance. There had been bitter sugar-
strikes in Jamaica and, when the play opened, it coincided most
conveniently with the publication of an official report on the
appalling economic and social conditions of the West Indies,
which effectively answered those critics who might have dis-
missed my case as wildly exaggerated propaganda. The press
notices were all I could have wished. They spoke of 'continuous
excitement', 'a good deal of humour' and 'real characters'. The
play ran to good houses through those hot, crisis-laden August
weeks. Unity was now ready to launch out in the West End
and it was agreed that *Colony* should be the first production.
It had to be lengthened and submitted to the Lord Chamberlain.
With Bert's help, and the experience of seeing the first version
acted before an audience, I made the required changes. The
censor raised no difficulties, the theatre was taken, the contract
signed, and a strong cast engaged, including Alfie Bass, Vida
Hope, John Slater and Bill Owen. Then, with the outbreak of
war, the whole project irretrievably collapsed.

For some time afterwards I was in touch with Bert, who
retained a gratifying faith in my abilities. When London's

theatrical life was resumed, after that brief (but, to my play, fatal) closure during the first weeks of the phoney war, Bert went to the Old Vic to direct modern plays. He urged me to write something new, something that it would be possible to produce under the changed conditions. I did not have to look far for inspiration.

In the months following Dunkirk the thought of invasion and occupation haunted most minds. How, I wondered, *would* one react, oneself? How ignobly would one behave? Suppose one steered a middle course between suicidal heroism and boot-licking collaboration (as the majority of any population would), how would one cope with an unavoidable moral crisis? The midnight knock would be terrible enough if it was a Gestapo man standing on the threshold, but that situation would leave little opportunity for personal decision. On the other hand, what if the man at the door was a fugitive patriot, a saboteur perhaps, and the penalty for sheltering him was torture and death, not merely for oneself but for one's family? What *was* a man's moral duty when, as did happen in occupied Europe, individual aid to the resistance movement brought massacre to an entire community?

This was the nightmare dilemma I wanted to write about. It was a theme I could explore only in imagination. At that date, early 1941, we had only a sketchy notion of what was happening in the countries the Nazis had just overrun. Later we were to have a spate of films and plays about the underground. None, to my knowledge, had then appeared, and when they did they were usually set in real, well-defined locations, France or Holland or even the Channel Islands.

It was the reactions of people like myself that concerned me, but an English background would have labelled the play defeatist. It seemed best once more to invent a country as I had invented an island for *Colony*. So I set my scene on a mountainous frontier, that could have been Norwegian or Czech or anywhere. I used the old device of a small assorted group of characters, isolated in a country inn, each with his or her complex background and problems, one of them to be revealed in due course as the traitor. The situation was one all too fresh in everybody's mind: carefree neutrality shattered suddenly by the Nazi violation of the frontier, and then the agonising individual dilemma demanding swift resolution, what am *I*, personally, going to do? What sort of a person *am* I? What men are these, whose example puts me to shame?

This was the imaginative problem I had to grapple with in my Cumberland room. Its remoteness from the war was quite illusory. The radio bulletins, the mealtime conversations, the boys' chatter and questions, the letters, the scraps of indirect news about friends and acquaintances, the newspaper maps, the little restrictions and austerities of daily life – all these kept the war constantly in one's mind. But the atmosphere was not that of the First World War. At this early stage people one knew were seldom in danger, still more rarely killed. My contemporaries, the over-thirties, were not fighter pilots or merchant seamen. The conscript soldier's turn had hardly come. Even the regulars, if they had survived the fall of France, were mostly stationed in Britain, waiting to repel an invasion if it came. The tension in our lives derived not from what *was* happening but from what *might*. The imagination could function as actively amid the deceptive quiet of the fells as anywhere else in the country.

The merits of *What Men Are These?* are now about as important as those of any lost Athenian drama beaten in the festival of 400 B.C. What happened is significant only in so far as it affected me, and my writing career, which is legitimate stuff for autobiography, and for what light it sheds upon the peculiar world of the theatre.

Bert received the play warmly. In the June of 1940 he had directed Robert Ardrey's inspiring *Thunder Rock* at the Neighbourhood Theatre. He sent me a printed copy. Under the cast of that first production, sparkling with names like Michael Redgrave and Bernard Miles, he wrote, 'For Geoffrey Trease, hoping to see *his* play prefaced by a record of its successful performance.' In a letter he added that Tyrone Guthrie had read my script, had made some criticism of the characterisation, but had otherwise praised it. Bert himself would like the first chance to direct it.

In the theatre, doubtless, things *can* happen quickly, but they are more likely to happen with agonising slowness, if at all. A publisher's office, while appearing a shade informal to the more conventional commercial eye, is a paragon of order and system compared with that of a theatrical management, at least as far as the consideration of manuscripts is concerned. There is a recognised process whereby a book can be submitted, read and rejected before the author dies of old age. It can be assumed also that, if the book is judged to be of publishable quality, and of the sort that accords with the firm's policy, it can be accepted promptly. Publication-date will depend on factors such as printing, binding and choice of season, but in general the publisher can see his way ahead. The factors governing a theatrical production are incalculable and sometimes bizarre. One may be the unpredictable date on which another play will finish and leave the theatre free. Another may be the pregnancy of the actress ideal for an important part. Theatrical finance is, to the outsider, a special mystery with its 'angels' or backers for individual shows. Their support may spring from pure devotion to drama or to a private understanding with some lady that she will only come to bed if she can also tread the boards. Even today, in well-known, publicly subsidised play-houses where there is some continuity of artistic policy, and many of these factors should not arise, the procedure for reading, reporting upon and returning unsolicited scripts compares poorly with that of a publisher's office. The theatre, like the law court, is a place of heart-breaking delay.

If one is not prepared to put up with it, one had better stay out. So, through the spring, summer and early autumn of 1941, I possessed myself in patience. I heard from Bert at intervals. He was putting out feelers in various quarters. But he could do nothing on his own.

In October I put the play in the hands of an agent, F. R. Steele, who had been a director of the famous J. B. Pinker & Son. I had already, in my impatience, authorised an amateur production by the Nottingham Philodramatic Society in their own little theatre in November. Steele saw no harm in this. Under the normal wartime conditions it might be a good thing. He might even get a 'film man' to go up to Nottingham and see it. Bert also talked of making the journey, thereby throwing some of the players into a flurry of expectation, unfortunately unfulfilled.

The one person who was certainly not going to see the performance was the author. I was anchored to my blackboard in
Cumberland, and there was not the slightest chance of getting
away. I could only write long letters to Marian, asking her to
be sure to send some flowers to the woman playing the lead,
and, if there was any sort of party afterwards, to chip in with
a bottle of something on my behalf. And then to let me know how
it all went.

It went well, apparently. Marian sent me a number of con-
gratulatory letters that had been addressed to her. One does
not, if wise, attach much weight to such messages, but when
they are unsolicited, and from people whose intellectual integrity one respects, they cannot help but raise one's spirits. Hilda
Lewis, the novelist, had been in the audience. She analysed the
play, act by act, thought it 'extremely interesting' and 'near to
being first-class', and spoke of its intensity and excitement.
Beryl Paston Brown, then a lecturer at Goldsmiths, evacuated
to Nottingham, described how she had gone home afterwards
with a group of friends and discussed the play till a late hour.
It raised 'so many issues of vital contemporary interest' that
she felt it 'bound to attract attention' wherever it was produced.

The fullest and frankest opinion came in a letter to myself
from a new friend whose judgement I had come to admire.
Gilbert Mockford was a rather sad figure, and indeed a tragic
one, as his suicide indicated, later in the war. He was a south-
erner, exiled by circumstances to Nottingham. He was cultivated
and discriminating. I shall never forget the occasion when he
sat down at his piano and introduced me to Couperin. Yet with
all his taste and intelligence he could support his family only
by churning out sentimental magazine fiction at so much per
thousand words. His drawing-room was a cultural oasis where,
once a week, he and his wife kept open house to any who would
brave the black-out. I used to go along with Marian during the
school holidays.

My play had come pat, he told me. 'I had to talk on recent
work in poetry, prose and drama, and you provided the evidence
that what I want to see in the theatre can be and is being done. . . .
The indifferent acting and production – some of the work was
dire – hardly mattered. The force of the play held the audience

tense, me with it. Able performers in a big theatre under competent direction would electrify. I wish you had been at the rehearsals to stir the actors' imaginations. . . . "Triumph of Playwright over Producer and Cast" is about the right headline for what I saw on Friday.' He went on at length with constructive criticism which seemed to me fair enough. But he concluded that I had written 'a play better than the theatre often sees and . . . as actual as yesterday afternoon or tomorrow morning'. In a separate letter to Marian he had written that it 'simply must get into the general theatre somehow. . . . Heavens, the thing is Box Office from start to finish, especially now, at this moment. Do tell me what is being done about it.'

She soon had hopeful news for him. Frank Steele was bestirring himself. A week later came a telegram from his office in the Haymarket: 'Have some interest being shown in What Men Are These which looks very promising. Keep me informed of your own activities and don't make any definite commitments without advising.' This was amplified by a letter just before Christmas.

> I have a manager definitely interested but he is just making arrangements to go into a new theatre and he asked me to leave it for a few days. I have told him that I do not want to leave it with him too long as I am very keen to get the play on in the West End and I have other managers in mind. . . . He asked me not to let anybody else even see it before he contacted me again which leads me to believe that we shall get together in a few days and discuss the matter.

Things seemed to be warming up. And in more ways than one. For contrapuntally, so to speak, to all this high drama of West End hopes something equally theatrical was developing in west Cumberland.

The school had been singularly free from the situations and scandals which, to judge from the light novels of that period, were so rife in the enclosed little communities of the private boarding school. But towards the end of that autumn term the emotional temperature had begun to rise.

First came the rumour, then the definite news, that the senior partner, the Major whom I had never seen, was returning to resume control. The older boys, remembering his prowess with the punishment slipper, licked their lips with apprehensive interest and petrified the listening juniors with their exaggerations. The assistant staff, divided between those who had worked under the Major and those who had not, speculated, hinted and watched the weather-signs.

I now hear for certain [I wrote home] that Major H. has applied for his discharge and hopes to be here before the end of term; that Mac has written to him that, if he returns, he himself will go – and has even sent in his resignation, which is not yet accepted. Apparently they had the most frightful rows in the old days. . . . The Major has written to Miss K., who of course will stick to the old school – and the winner. I imagine the Matron won't stay, and even my informant (the housekeeper) seems dubious about her future. Drama! I hope I can stay to see it. I don't see how I could leave myself, unless called up, without a term's notice, except by mutual agreement. God knows how the Major would staff the school under present conditions.

The much-awaited day – and the legendary Major – duly arrived. Mac had already vacated the best bedroom. At the first meal together he had moved from the head of the table to the opposite end.

The Major proved to be an extrovert of sanguine temperament and appearance, whom it was easy to picture as Entertainments Officer at Catterick or wherever it was he had been. He was an enthusiastic music-lover. He told me he had been one of the first – possibly he said *the* first – to 'discover' Eileen Joyce. This interesting statement I have never been able to check. He took no part in the teaching and for a few days the life of the school continued without alteration. I observed him with guarded interest. Whatever his shortcomings might prove to be, I had to admit that his advent had brought a gust of fresh air into our hermetic little household. Then one day when I was alone in the cottage he tapped on the sitting-room door.

'You know Mac's leaving?'

'So I understand, sir.'

'He insists. Now, I shall want *you* to act as headmaster.'

Taken by surprise, I could only warn him that I had passed my army medical and was expecting call-up at any time.

'I can't spare you,' he said magnificently. 'I shall have a word with our M.P.' Having just quit the King's service himself, he seemed little troubled by the thought of depriving His Majesty of another man. I did not believe that his influence would affect my future one way or the other, so I did not argue. The Major was not a man to argue with unnecessarily. There would be sufficient arguments later, no doubt, if I were left for another term there and had to adjust myself to this new arrangement.

So, in those last days of the autumn term, while unknown to the school my agent was working to transform me into a West End playwright, a little comedy developed at Gosforth.

The staff had a whip-round to buy Mac a parting gift. Fur driving-gloves, decreed the riding-mistress. I went to White-haven with her to choose them. Meanwhile, as he had known my work far longer than the Major was likely to, Mac gave me a warm testimonial, proclaiming, as employers are apt to do, a far rosier opinion of my character and abilities than he had ever previously betrayed.

The climax of the comedy was the last day of term. The parents assembled to collect their boys. The Major made a speech. He had to announce with deep regret that his partner was leaving. Though unfit for military service he felt that in this period of national emergency he must take some more direct part in the war effort. Everybody was sorry, but such a decision must be respected. Parents could rest assured that the school would continue . . . etcetera.

The epilogue came at New Year. The Major wrote me an apologetic letter. Now that he had been into everything, he could not face the unfamiliar problems of running a school under war-time restrictions. So it was he, after all, who would be leaving, and Mac had agreed to return.

The news lost much of its impact because I was receiving far more interesting letters from Steele. The manager he had previously mentioned had just 'suggested that we meet him at the theatre at 6 o'clock on Monday or Tuesday'. It was a stroke of

fortune that I had another two weeks of holiday. Full of cautious
optimism, I caught the London train.

That evening glitters brightly in my memory. The theatre
was the Whitehall. The Anglo-Polish ballet was playing to
packed houses – ballet was one of the great popular British
discoveries of the war. Steele was a kindly man with a lifelong
experience of the theatre. He had a slight limp and was stocky
in build. But it is his personality and what he said that remains
vivid, along with all other details of that encounter.

Mr Buckmaster greeted me with *empressement*. He had read
my play and liked it. His wife had read it – and liked it. He paid
great attention to his wife's opinion. He had always found it
wise to do so. Then, with me following goggle-eyed at his
heels, he took us on a tour of the theatre. He would fling open
a swing-door, to reveal – furnace-like – a hot interior, boiling
with rapt humanity, vibrant Slavonic music that almost knocked
you back again, and, in the distance, bright as fire, the illuminated stage and its whirling performers. Blandly indifferent to
those of the audience within earshot, he would inform us in a
loud voice, 'This is the Circle. When we play to capacity this
grosses – ' so many pounds. Then we walked out again, went
up or down a flight of stairs, entered another part of the auditorium and were told its significance in box-office terms. It was
embarrassing but exquisitely exciting.

Leaving the ballet-lovers to enjoy themselves without further
interruption, we adjourned to the deserted bar and I sat on the
upholstered bench between them, mutely sipping my drink
while they bandied practical details over my elated head.

'Go slow on film-rights till we see if we can get a Broadway
production as well – '

'Yes, get far more for them if we have a Broadway offer
first – '

Point after point. Percentages, grosses. . . . Everything
seemed deliciously harmonious between them.

'Did you have anyone special in mind?'

I realised with a start that I was being drawn into the conference. 'Er?'

'The casting,' they explained kindly. Had I been thinking of
any particular stars? They were anxious to meet my wishes.

Thus encouraged, I ventured the names of Michael Redgrave and Margaret Rawlings. It would be wonderful if. . . .

It was agreed that my suggestions were sensible and well within the bounds of possibility.

I do not think we drank much as we sat there – my companions were far too intent on their business discussion – but if I had consumed a bottle of champagne unaided I could not have left the theatre in a more exalted mood.

In the blacked-out street Frank Steele detected an approaching taxi, hailed it and bundled me in.

'Is it going to be all right?' I demanded.

'Well, you know, nothing's ever certain till a contract's signed.'

'I know, but – with *your* long experience – '

'I'd say it's in the bag.'

A week or two later I was back in Gosforth. Life there resumed as if the Major had never been. His plans for me had never, I think, been widely known. Between Mac and myself there was no embarrassment, for there had never been any conflict. He kept his driving-gloves, I kept his testimonial, we all kept quiet about the situation with which the previous term had ended.

It was a bitter month, that January of 1942. The train that took me round the Cumbrian coast was the last to get through for a fortnight. The next, a goods train, was buried by a landslide and the line remained blocked. Until it was cleared, and our luggage came through, I had little more than the clothes I stood up in. There was snow everywhere and my shoes leaked. I caught a bad chill and for a week or more languished in bed. The village doctor asked me if I had ever had malaria and seemed puzzled when I said no. Fortunately my trunk had come through by then, for I sometimes had to change into dry pyjamas in the middle of the night. It was a long time before I could crawl back to the classroom.

On 2 February, Steele wrote:

I am still waiting for definite news from Buckmaster with regard to *What Men Are These?* I understand his principal backer lives about fifty miles out and usually comes up by

car and the explanation is that he won't risk it while the
roads are so bad. We have been having a great deal of snow
here lately. I have been on continuously because I was hoping
that we should be able to proceed long before this. As you
know, I sent a full agreement and have been awaiting any
suggested revisions before submitting it to you for approval. I
telephoned Margaret Rawlings, who is now on farm work,
but I understand that she does not feel inclined to give up
this farm work for the theatre for the duration. However, I
think if we got a contract signed that I might approach her
again because she would be a good draw. . . .

I had it under consideration with somebody else but after
hearing again from Buckmaster that he expected to have the
agreement completed within 48 hours, I withdrew it from
the other people to avoid complications. I am getting very
impatient myself and I know you must be also.

He was right there. I could only set my teeth and, being now
recovered enough to sit down to my typewriter, concentrate on
some revisions that had been agreed. On 18 February Steele
wrote to acknowledge their receipt and to say he was having
fresh copies typed. There was now a real note of anxiety in his
tone.

I have told Buckmaster that we cannot give him any longer
than this week to come to a definite decision. . . . Buckmaster
is still very keen indeed and enthusiastic but he is still waiting
for his principal to come to town, but as I told him, it is not
much use to any of us if there is to be further delay.

February passed into March. Whether the unknown angel
ever braved the frosty roads and reached London, I never knew.
The indefatigable Steele wrote that he had 'several people
interested in the play' but still no definite decision. 'Firth Shepherd agrees that it is a good play, but his strong conviction is
that the subject is too depressing to find favour among audiences
today. . . . We of course do not agree with this view and hope
to prove him completely in the wrong.'

One day I was on duty in the little wood where the boys loved to potter and build dens. Mac came out, shouting that I was wanted on the telephone.

I hurried indoors. It was not Steele but Marian. My call-up papers had arrived in Nottingham. I was to report at Carlisle Castle in ten days.

Mac behaved very decently. He released me at once so that I could spend those days with my family. The boys gathered outside the cottage when I left for the station. My last memory is of seeing, with astonishment, that one of the older boys was openly weeping.

CHAPTER FIVE

The King's Own

MARCH 19, 1942 provided me with a private anniversary rather like Pepys's 26 March 1658, when he had that gruesome operation for the stone. I do not, like Pepys, celebrate it with a party. When it recurs, I merely feel a chill draught of recollection. 'This was the day. . . . '

All through the previous night I had dozed fitfully in a third-class railway-compartment, blinds drawn against the Nazi bombers. The stations were ghostly with subdued lights, the long desolate platforms had the hollow echo of the small hours. Crewe, Warrington, Wigan, Preston, Lancaster . . . then, in the dawn, Carlisle. I handed in my one-way ticket and walked out into the waking town.

The big station-hotel gave me a splendid breakfast. With wistful memories of that meal, I went back a week or two later. The doorman barred my way. 'Can't you see the notice? Out of bounds to Other Ranks!'

After my last civilian meal I walked up to the Castle to report. I was not to enjoy even the consolation of serving within that history-laden fortress. Soon I was driving out of its grim gateway again, jammed inside a covered truck with a pack of other conscripts, going we knew not where. It was a symbolic introduction to our new life: discomfort, crowding, and not a glimpse of what lay ahead.

In a few minutes we reached the training-camp outside the town. For the next forty-eight hours we were on a conveyor-belt which stripped us stage by stage of all individuality as remorselessly as it stripped away the last shred of our own clothing. This went into a sandbag and was sent home. A macabre procedure. I felt halfway already to being a name on a war memorial.

I was now 3718908 Private Trease, R. (what did a man want with a second Christian name?) of the King's Own Royal Regiment. I was 'the King's own' all right, to do as he pleased with. 'Private' was ironical indeed. I had been robbed of my identity and issued with identity discs instead. Where was the person who, a few months ago, had sat in a theatre listening to talk of Broadway and film rights? Not for the first time in my life I was back to Square One, but this time, in the new argot I had to learn, I was bashing it.

Army slang was fresh to me, an enriching linguistic experience, and my notebook collected many picturesque expressions, mainly related to sexual activity. To knock a round off, have a nibble, dip it in, and have a bit of hearthrug pie, were just four phrases not to be found in Roget. The jargon of authority was another matter, and to me one of the minor horrors of war. 'Eighteen hundred-hours' pained the pedant in me, even when it meant liberation. I resented being ordered to violate grammar and 'get fell in'. To a writer it was like being made to spit on the flag. It seemed inopportune, however, to protest to the sergeant.

I was in a hut with men mainly of my own age, drawn from Cumberland and Lancashire. Rough of speech, they were touchingly gentle of manner and though I was obviously the odd man out I was never made to suffer for it. Incongruously in that chain-gang situation I was sometimes addressed as 'Mr' Trease.

As a writer I look back gratefully on that enlarging experience, for ordinarily I should never have known, really known, such men. I could never, for instance, have conceived a character like 'Willy the Waller', the semi-illiterate Cumbrian workman, whose adventures as a soldier during the collapse of France provided the central core of my plot in *Black Banner Abroad* twelve years later. Observation of my comrades could even be transferred, *mutatis mutandis*, to characterisation in historical stories. Shakespeare could have drawn those camp-fire groups on the eve of Agincourt from the men in my squad.

After sixteen weeks of basic training I never saw any of them again, yet they remain vivid. There was Wilf Snape, cotton-mill clerk, who could talk standard English to me and switch instantaneously into broad Lancashire with the others. There was Murtagh, the bellicose Liverpool Irishman. There was young Douglas, our only nineteen-year-old, as much our pet as he was his mother's. After his first visit home he convulsed us with his imitation of her shocked reaction to his military crop. 'Ee, *Douglas*, what ha' they done to thi *hair*?' We went about chortling for days, imitating his imitation. 'Ee, *Dooglas*, what ha' they done to thi *hair*?' We laughed easily, welcoming every chance.

And there was Bradley, for whom 'cunning little runt' was the inevitable description, whose very slyness made him slightly endearing, like a servant in opera. One day the squad was clustered round a Bren gun. The sergeant demonstrated how it could jam at an awkward moment. 'Now,' he said, 'suppose the Jerries are coming at you with the bayonet. They're only ten yards away. Bradley, what would you do?'

'Bugger off quick, sergeant,' was the honest reply.

'You wouldn't,' I said, 'you'd stay and sell them the gun.'

Even the horrendous Sergeant-Major Tripp managed a twinkle for Bradley. Once we were set to dig an apparently pointless hole. Tripp strutted over to inspect it, his bulldog face deadpan. Bradley asked, 'What'll I do wi' all these sods, sir? Bury 'em?' and Tripp said, 'Not on your life, Bradley. I'll want 'em on parade in the morning.'

When Lights Out sounded sweetly on a distant bugle, and we snuggled under our blankets in the long hut with its appalling fug of rank cigarettes, sweat and coke-fumes, it would be Bradley we should hear intoning obscene verses in the dark.

Army life was at once better and worse than I had expected. Physically, it was testing. Walking was the only form of exercise I had ever really enjoyed, and I had been thankful to finish with games at school. I was now thirty-two. So, while the drill came back to me and the marching held no terrors, I was not happy in the gym or on the assault-course, clambering over high obstacles and swinging from ropes. Nor, remembering my boyhood ineptness with a cricket ball, did I enjoy throwing live hand-grenades. Somehow my instructor and I survived.

The King's Own was immensely proud of its seniority among the infantry of the line. We were the 4th Foot, one of the Tan-

gier regiments raised under Charles II, with a 'Lion of England'
cap-badge, mercifully simple and responsive to polish, dating
from our first battle-honour at Namur in 1695. Early in my
training we had a gala week, involving compulsory attendance
at three boxing contests, two football matches and a ceremonial
church parade on St George's Day, with the officers and sergeants sporting roses in their caps. This packed programme of
entertainment was supposed to heighten our morale. The effect
on me was irritation and depression, for it robbed me of precious hours of liberty which alone kept me sane.

My instinct, which became almost obsessive, was to get out
of camp at the earliest permissible moment and to stay out until
I could escape the other way, into blessed sleep. My one refuge
inside the gates was the Y.M.C.A. which, unlike the N.A.A.F.I.
canteen, recognised that some people preferred unsugared tea. I
made friends with the warden, Miss Redmayne, and some of
her volunteer helpers, and became for an hour an individual
again. There too I met my first Education Sergeant, Clitheroe,
who came out from the Castle to give us classical gramophone
concerts. It was to prove a useful contact.

There were other canteens in the town. The Catholic Women
served the best sausage-and-chip suppers, Toc H catered for
the quiet minority. I could get a bath at Toc H, and the sympathetic warden, Charles Young, gave me the use of a typewriter. Marian was handling any literary business that cropped
up, but sometimes there was a letter only I could answer.
Steele was persevering in his attempts to get my play a try-out,
but he had no luck. From New York James Henle of Vanguard
wrote enthusiastically, asking about me and my work, and
reporting that he had arranged for a school edition of *Cue for
Treason* in Canada. These rare reminders of my true identity
were reassuring. One or two precious civilian contacts in
Carlisle reinforced them. Thomas Gray, the public librarian,
asked me to supper. And through one of Marian's friends I was
sent an introduction to a schoolmistress who lodged only a mile
from the camp. In her sitting-room, over her landlady's coffee
and sandwiches, fruit tart and parkin, I could talk of Greek
literature and other topics remote from the barrack-room. It was
Miss Tinkler who introduced me to Noel Streatfeild's *Ballet*

Shoes, a book which delighted me and was a salutary indication that other people were working towards a better children's literature in a way, and with a motivation, quite different from my own. I noted *Ballet Shoes* as a story that Jocelyn would soon be old enough to enjoy, and must not miss.

After some weeks we had intelligence tests and an interview. 'I find you rather a problem,' said the Major. 'Have you thought about a commission?'

I told him of my earlier volunteering. Now, mindful of the stringent demands being made on the new type of officer, I had lost confidence in my adequacy. I was coping with my present training – just. 'But nowadays', I said, 'it seems that an officer must not only be able to swim crocodile-infested rivers but tow his platoon after him as well.'

He smiled. 'How old are you?'

'Nearly thirty-three, sir.'

'Perhaps you're right.' He suggested the Intelligence Corps, but I had only one of the two modern languages required. Finally he put me down for the Army Educational Corps, but without any guarantee that I would get into it.

I had been attracted by what I had heard of the A.E.C. even before entering the Army, and its local sergeant had told me a little more. I knew it was a very small corps, a yeast activating the whole military mixture. Its origins went right back to Sir John Moore, the Corunna hero, when the development of the rifle and light-infantry tactics provoked the astonishing new thought that the best soldiers were not necessarily stupid automata, standing in close formation to be shot at, but intelligent individuals who knew what they were doing. This revolutionary doctrine had made slow progress even by 1942, but in almost a century and a half the Serjeant-Schoolmasters of the Napoleonic wars had evolved first into the Corps of Army Schoolmasters and then, when Churchill was at the War Office in 1920, into the Army Educational Corps. Now, in the unprecedented circumstances of the Second World War, the role of the Corps had been vastly extended. It was accepted that the new conscript armies would fight better if they knew what they were fighting for. The Army Council had set up in 1941 the Army Bureau of Current Affairs to help the Corps, and even the

most red-necked Blimp paid lip-service to the value of talks and
discussion-groups. They were less enthusiastic about the gramophone recitals, the lectures on popular science, the classes in
leatherwork and soft-toy-making, the play-readings and historical excursions. But they realised that the troops had to be
occupied somehow until the Second Front opened, and these
various diversions were at least better than V.D.

The Corps operated in a sort of skeleton formation. Its members worked largely alone, a sergeant or warrant-officer being
attached to some big military unit or even having a whole area
to cover. He seldom met fellow-members of the A.E.C. Mainly
he worked, as diplomatically as possible, with the unit education
officer who was himself an infantryman, a gunner, R.A.O.C. or
in some other main branch of the service. In practice the A.E.C.
instructor was very much a lone wolf, a combination of salesman,
missionary and political commissar. If he was lucky, he might
be given a little unqualified assistance from some junior N.C.O.
in the unit.

My hopes soared when, late that May, I was sent on a week's
course for part-time assistants of this kind. Such a course might
be a stepping-stone to the Corps itself. I was temporarily
transformed into an acting unpaid lance-corporal and, laden like
a pack-mule with my four blankets, rifle and the rest of my kit,
started on the awkward cross-country train-journey to the Army
School of Education at Love Lane, Wakefield. The address
sounded more glamorous than it proved. Love Lane was shadowed by the formidable façade of Wakefield Prison. The School,
itself a pleasant-enough building, was the peace-time home of
the prison officers.

That week was a green oasis in a desert year. The food and
living conditions were civilised: even to share one's room with
only one other man was a luxury. The week's programme was
stimulating, and so was the company, mostly teachers in civil
life. The officer-instructors treated us as intelligent human beings
and social equals. The doyen was a Major Insh, who looked
about eighty-five, a kind of Mr Chips in khaki, who went
everywhere with a luggage-label fluttering from his respirator,
a safeguard (we assumed) against loss of memory. Local history
was his speciality. He doddered gamely up to Sandal Castle and

expounded the tactics at the Battle of Wakefield. We speculated as to whether he was the last eye-witness. It was easy to
smile at him, impossible not to like him, especially when he
congratulated me on my first little book for adults, *Walking in
England*, which he had run to earth in the public library. The
other officers were younger but equally sympathetic.

There was music, a private tour of the local art gallery,
demonstrations on discussion-group and other techniques, and
specimen lecturettes which we had to prepare and deliver. Using
my 1935 experiences, I talked on 'The Russian Man-in-the-
street'. My tutor advised me to apply for transfer to the A.E.C.
as soon as I got back to Carlisle. Wakefield would give me a
strong recommendation.

After such a week, Carlisle was like a ghost's return at cock-
crow. To don those filthy denims, get fell in, and resume all the
childish routine was worse than ever.

I promptly put in for transfer, but found myself up against a
blank wall. Such things were governed by A.C.I.s, Army
Council Instructions, and the relevant one stipulated that
applicants must be thirty-three on 1 August. My birthday – in
which Sergeant-Major Tripp showed a sudden, uncharacter-
istic and far from benign interest – fell on 11 August. My
application could not go forward.

I despaired, but only temporarily. I knew I had found the one
army job I could do effectively. Rules could be bent – by the
pulling of strings. Everyone else did it. I must try to learn how.

The new A.E.C. sergeant at the Castle consulted his officer.
I was advised to write to my tutor at Wakefield. Protocol had
formerly forbidden this. Now, with that most precious thing,
'an officer's permission', I could do so. A remoter string was
tweaked by a lawyer friend in London. He knew a Labour peer
at G.H.Q. *He* put in an inquiry to the Under-Secretary, who
(the whisper came back to me) had asked for the file with my
particulars. But the weeks passed and my infantry training came
to an end. I had survived with only minor ailments, but the
M.O. was not impressed with my condition and there was talk
of sending me to a convalescent home at Skegness to put on
some weight.

On the final morning we marched into Carlisle. For the next

few nights we had to sleep on the shelves of the linen-room at the Crown and Mitre, 'on draft' to one of the regiment's battalions. We never knew from one hour to the next when, or where, we should go. We were continually paraded in a back-street outside the Territorial drill-hall to comply with some fresh formality. Then, when I had given up all expectation of reprieve, came the parade when a voice barked: 'Trease!'

'Sir?'

'Fall out an' report to the Orderly Sar'n't!'

In the drill-hall, in a partitioned cubbyhole, a genial sergeant and his plump corporal welcomed me as their new dogsbody. I had been taken off the draft until the King's pleasure should be known, and was to work partly for them, partly for the Education Sergeant.

The drill-hall was a place through which men passed briefly on their return from hospital, detention or absence without leave, before they were posted elsewhere. Their beds filled the hall. The sergeant told me to find a vacant one for myself and keep a sharp eye on my possessions. 'That lot', he said, 'can steal the socks you've got on, without removing your boots.' I found a bed on the stage at the end, and in fact lost nothing.

We kept a card-index of this floating population, but in a light-hearted manner. The corporal would scrutinize a card in puzzlement. 'This bloke gone? Has he ever arrived? Anyone *seen* him? Then I reckon he don't exist.' The card was dropped into the waste-paper basket. Sometimes, in extremes of misery, I had toyed with the fantasy of desertion. This might have been a good place from which to vanish.

Life now was easy. We welcomed arrivals, dispensed information, obtained travel warrants, arranged sick parades and appointments with the 'trick cyclist'. We lurked behind our partition, ruminating and reminiscing over mugs of tea. I continued to enlarge my knowledge of the common man. If I felt like a change, I had only to say that I was wanted by the Education Sergeant at the Castle. Sometimes I was. At others I went quietly to ground in the public library, which lay conveniently on my route. Who said that a man could not serve two masters? There is nothing like it.

Marian and Jocelyn came up for a few days. My friendly

schoolmistress was away on holiday, so we were able to take over her lodgings and I obtained a sleeping-out pass. On our wedding anniversary I was particularly anxious to get away from the drill-hall in good time. A malign fate decreed that on that one day I should be delayed by a routine anti-gas test. But in the orderly sergeant's cubbyhole I had learned how to deal with such tiresome emergencies. I skipped the parade and forged the necessary entry in my pay-book. Then, with all the guilty glee of the normally law-abiding person, I slipped away to the family reunion.

Marian opened the door herself with gratifying promptness. 'We're all right, darling,' she said quickly, 'we weren't hurt.'

Mystified I followed her into the sitting-room. I saw that she was pale. 'What on earth – ?' I began.

'You haven't heard? I thought you might have seen the evening paper.'

I knew that they had been planning a bus-ride to Langholm, so that Jocelyn could say she had been to Scotland. Over tea, Marian told me what had happened. She left some details until later. Jocelyn was not yet six.

Sweeping round a bend in the Esk valley their bus had met a truck full of soldiers. At that point the road hugged a precipitous hillside, forty feet above the river. The bus had crashed through a wall, somersaulted, and landed on its roof at the water's edge. They had scrambled out, cut and dazed. A line of men had materialised, strung down the slope, a human chain helping them to safety, First Aid, and cups of sweet tea at the local big house. Marian herself had barely taken it in, it had happened so quickly. She hoped that Jocelyn had not seen the dead and injured. The dead included a girl who had moved into their seat when they changed sides to get a better view.

They themselves had suffered no serious hurt, though Marian was to feel the delayed effects for a long time afterwards. That evening, seeing them both apparently well and cheerful, I could not myself absorb the full significance of their experience. My own shock, and it was momentarily numbing, came the next evening when I saw the photograph in the paper – the inverted bus stretched along the edge of what was described as 'one of the deepest salmon pools in the river'.

Marian and Jocelyn returned to Nottingham. The weeks went by. I fell ill with shingles and languished in the sick bay in the Castle. I crawled back to duty. Was I to stay for ever in the drill-hall, card-indexing other forgotten men?

Suddenly, action. 'Trease!' bawled the corporal with unwonted urgency. 'Get up to the Castle quick – brigadier's waitin' for you on the square. Best take my bike.'

The brigadier was the top man in the A.E.C. He was touring Western Command with the colonel from headquarters at Chester.

I stood on the pedals and urged the olive-green monstrosity up the cobbled approach to the Castle gateway. I saw the two imposing figures, their caps encircled with the Cambridge blue of the Corps instead of the commoner scarlet. The unit education officer and the A.E.C. sergeant were in attendance. I almost fell off the too-large bicycle, threw it against a convenient expanse of medieval masonry, stamped my feet absurdly, the A.E.C. being always anxious that its members should look like real soldiers, and saluted with vibrating keenness. The brigadier turned to the colonel and said pleasantly:

'I think we might constitute ourselves a selection board on the spot, don't you?'

They interrogated me for five minutes. It chanced that the colonel was not only an Oxford man but had also been to Queen's. 'Have you never regretted going down without a degree?' he asked.

'Not until lately, sir. It never occurred to me it could possibly affect my military career.'

This seemed to divert them. 'This man's application is to go forward,' said the brigadier.

I was sorry that Sergeant-Major Tripp was not there to hear. But I had passed out of his ken, and I doubt if he ever knew or cared that I had circumvented his sacred A.C.I.

A month later I was posted to Wakefield for the transfer course. On the last day of October I replaced the King's Own cap-badge with the open book and crossed weapons of the Army Educational Corps and stitched the three stripes of a sergeant-instructor on all my sleeves.

THE second scene of *Macbeth* opens, as every schoolboy knows, with the entrance of 'a bleeding Sergeant'. Duncan turns to his staff and asks (rudely, we used to think): 'What bloody man is that?' The situation neatly paralleled the arrival of an A.E.C. sergeant newly posted to a unit that viewed him with suspicion and did not quite know what to do with him. Shakespeare's sergeant even continues the parallel by launching immediately, exhausted though he is, into an eloquent exposition of Current Affairs.

After a ten-day course at Wakefield we were dispatched in all directions, nearly a hundred of us, the largest intake in the history of the Corps. Few of us were likely to meet again. Ours was essentially a solitary job.

I myself was posted to the 31st Battalion of the Royal Warwickshires at Coventry, a sad grey city that November, a year after the bombing. The battalion was scattered round the perimeter in detachments of various sizes, guarding a civil airfield, a factory, an ammunition dump, or anything that could be regarded as a military objective. I soon saw that this was a face-saving device. Battalions with numbers like that, 30th and 31st, were very different from the fighting battalions higher in the list. They were composed of 'category men' with medical grades less than A.1. How they would have dealt with a parachutist attack on the objective they were guarding would be ungenerous of me, as their one-time guest, to speculate. Their powers of resistance to education, at least, were strong.

I reported to battalion headquarters, where the R.S.M.'s welcome barely paraphrased Duncan's query. The unit education officer was informed. Some fairly junior officer did this job, not usually considered very vital. Again I found myself in the con-

venient position of serving two masters. I must work under
Lieutenant Hadley, a zealous little man, who, having other and
more pressing regimental duties, had to give me a free hand.
My other master was the Staff Officer Education at Central
Midland District in Leamington Spa, nine miles away. To him
I must submit a written fortnightly report. For an individualist
there could have been few more congenial jobs in the Army.

'I'm afraid there's no room for you here in the sergeants'
mess,' Mr Hadley explained. 'You'll be quartered with one of
the detachments. At Howes Lane. I'll drive you there now.'

I was not sorry. I had no desire to be in the mess at headquarters, under the R.S.M.'s eye, and there were similar advantages in keeping a mile or two between Hadley and myself.

As he drove me round the dark by-roads he made it clear that
I was highly privileged to be attached to the Warwicks, Mont-
gomery's old regiment and the sixth of the line. Such things
were important.

'Yes, sir,' I said, adding casually, '*We* were very proud of our
seniority in the King's Own. Being the Fourth of Foot.'

Hadley and I were to have our little brushes, but on the whole
we got on well, and I was sad to hear, much later, that he had
been killed in Italy.

The little camp to which he delivered me was a mere cluster
of Nissen huts in a dank field adjoining a factory near Whitley
Abbey. In daylight the setting was revealed as ruined-rural,
with a belt of dejected leafless woodland contrasted with the
hard lines of workshop roofs and tall chimney. Night or day,
it seemed always bleak, foggy and unlovely.

If I was Macbeth's 'bleeding Sergeant', this detachment might
have been cast for those 'tattered prodigals' in *Henry IV*, who
stung Falstaff to object, 'I'll not march through Coventry with
them, that's flat.' There was no officer. There were two sergeants, both beery old regulars, the fatherly and sentimental
'Jenky' and the hatchet-faced, humorous George. George was
provost-sergeant, concerned mainly with defaulters. He struck
me as a poacher turned gamekeeper.

With this pair I was to share what passed for the Sergeants'
Mess. It was just a Nissen hut, divided into living-space and
sleeping-quarters by a blanket hung across the middle. We

naturally had no cook of our own, still less a bar, which was
perhaps as well, for Jenky and George had an unfathomable
capacity for beer, as I found when I sometimes accompanied
them on a sociable evening in the town. An orderly brought us
massive platefuls from the cook-house, washed up, tended the
stove, and woke us each morning with a mug of tea. It was not
Wakefield, but neither was it Carlisle.

I grew quite fond of my two companions, and, though they
must have considered me an odd character, with incomprehensible
interests and duties, they showed a friendly tolerance. George
had a refreshing flow of vigorous idioms, delivered in a deadpan
manner, which often delighted me. Once Jenky came into the
hut and mentioned that there was a young woman at the gate
closely questioning the sentry about the present whereabouts
of a man recently posted elsewhere. Jenky made some naïve
comment. George set down his mug with a scornful thump and
retorted: 'Shatter my tonsils, if that gal's not in the pudding-
club, my prick's a bloater!'

Coventry was a tragic, numb place that winter. There were
just three cafés where I could find some sort of a meal on
Saturday afternoons – until the eggs and the toasted cheese
gave out and the doors were bolted against further customers.
There were cinemas, true, and the Hippodrome, and occasionally
in the Technical College theatre I might see the Ballet Rambert
or a touring company in *Hedda Gabler*. The public library had
been destroyed in the blitz.

At Howes Lane I worked in a corner of another hut. I had a
typewriter, a trestle table, a supply of paper, and a pile of
pamphlets. A filthy stove scattered large smuts everywhere. The
air was constantly full of twirling specks, so that at first I
imagined I was liverish. Without a single drawer or cupboard
it was hard to protect anything.

I was usually glad to get out and visit the other detachments.
Distances were short and I could cover them on a bicycle. The
enterprising Hadley disturbed me from time to time with the
murmured suggestion that a motorcycle would save my time,
but to my relief there was a shortage of machines and for once
I was thankful that education had so low a priority. I was
unmechanical and had long believed that the invention of the

internal combustion engine had been one of mankind's most retrograde steps. Motorcycles alarmed me more than, at that safe distance, all the combined hordes of Germany and Japan.

A.E.C. sergeants were like lonely parsons wished upon apathetic parishes. How much work we did depended on our initiative and diplomacy. Faced with an indifferent or hostile C.O., adjutant or sergeant-major, we were impotent. We could run round with a few drawing-pins, arranging displays and wall-newspapers, but talks and discussions were impossible if we were not allowed the 'bodies' for an hour or two.

It was hard to fill a week with the battalion alone, so I also visited some of the anti-aircraft batteries ringing the city. This was more rewarding. The gunners were more intelligent, and, as these were 'mixed' batteries, half my audience were girls of the A.T.S. or Auxiliary Territorial Service, as the Women's Royal Army Corps was then called.

The girls were always more responsive to cultural subjects. For them I first worked out a programme called 'A Play Is Born'. Using my own *After the Tempest* as an example, I discussed the factors governing the creation of a stage-play, drawing suggestions and answers from the audience as I went along, in the manner taught us at Wakefield. Then, having laid all the jigsaw pieces before them, I showed them the finished picture by giving a one-man recital of the whole thing. The complete programme fitted comfortably into the sixty minutes allowed, and as there were numerous lines and situations that a mixed military audience could grasp instantly and with glee it proved a popular feature.

The same basic idea was no less useful to me in a quite different connection.

Round about this date the National Book League began to promote Children's Book Weeks in public libraries. Exhibitions, competitions and other activities were combined with talks by authors and illustrators, and parties were brought from all the local schools. I was asked to speak at Islington and, as Hadley was willing to issue an overnight pass, I was able to accept. But what to talk about to these children? Encouraged by the success of my programme with the troops, I worked out a similar talk, 'A Book Is Born', explaining how my stories evolved step by step from the first notebook jotting to a completed typescript. The tedium of a long lecture, to which they were quite un-accustomed, could be avoided by involving the young audience in a question-and-answer procedure from the start. I obviously could not end by reading them the book, so I spent the rest of my time, until the concluding free-for-all question-period, deal-ing with the fate of the manuscript after it reached the publisher. Children, I was to learn, were fascinated to hear about con-tracts, royalties, conflicts with illustrators, and the like, while examples of printers' errors, such as 'For Sale, Alsatian pup pies', would have them rolling in the aisles.

It was good to be in London again, even a war-time London of bricked-up windows and sandbagged doorways under a pewter-grey February sky hung with barrage-balloons. It was my first visit since that evening in the bar at the Kingsway Theatre when the mirage of West End glory had shimmered before my eyes. Now, for an hour or two, I was an author again. There were my books on display at the library, including the newly pub-lished one I had written in Cumberland. And there to hear my talk was a woman from the B.B.C. schools department, who mentioned that *The Grey Adventurer* was to be broadcast, and I should be getting an offer through my publishers.

The talk itself went well. I gave it to sixty boys and girls at two o'clock. At five to three they clattered out and another sixty came in. I repeated my talk. I was still to be repeating it, with variations, thirty years later. I was to give it hundreds of times in half the counties of England and to English-speaking children as far away as Athens. Like a music-hall artist I was to meet no two audiences the same. Each had to be assessed at sight, probed with the first joke, wooed at the right speed and with the right degree of subtlety. There were wooden audiences and incandescent ones, tough unbookish lads and starry-eyed High School juniors, children who were rather too young for it and rebellious adolescents who thought themselves too old. Sometimes the questions came spontaneous as hail. At others they had to be drawn almost painfully, at first, like teeth. The only audience that ever baffled me was that at an old-fashioned girls' boarding-school, where a dragonlike headmistress faced them from the platform and inhibited them from opening their mouths. Normally there was not much inhibition. 'How old are you?' 'Are you married?' 'How much do you earn?' 'How many books have you had *rejected?*' I learned to be ready for any question.

These talks by children's authors were then a new thing in Britain, though I had heard of them seven or eight years earlier in Russia, where all kinds of bright schemes seemed to be afoot in the public libraries and Pioneer Palaces. It was good to see the experiment taken up, however modestly, in Britain. As a means of encouraging the unbookish child to read, and of stimulating other children to extend the range of their interests, it was demonstrably effective. It occurred to me that war-time Britain was belatedly following the Russians in a number of respects, others being the encouragement of married women to work and the provision of crèches, kindergartens and canteens.

I was reminded of Russia in a less agreeable manner when I went on to Portland Place, where Muriel Burton, friend of my Bloomsbury days in hack journalism, was now working in the B.B.C. Variety Department. The keen scrutiny of the hall-porters and the paraphernalia of passes to get in and out of the various buildings were all too reminiscent of Moscow in 1935.

Up in Room 703, once I was permitted to get there, the atmosphere was more welcoming. Muriel's chief, Brandreth, was in normal times a theatre-manager with a taste for experimental plays. Meeting him fanned my hopes to life again. He asked for a copy of *What Men Are These?*, and later Frank Steele, who knew him well, passed on his comments: 'I think it is an extremely good piece of work, and Val Gielgud also thinks well of it, but does not consider it would make a good radio play. . . . If I had been running Richmond, this is without doubt a play which we should have staged there.' The story of any would-be dramatist can be told almost entirely in those two words, 'if' and 'but'.

The real pleasure of that London visit, though, was not in any serious resurgence of my theatrical ambitions but in the brief escape from the military atmosphere. To stroll down Charing Cross Road and enjoy the bookshops again . . . to meet Muriel for lunch next day at a Greek restaurant in Percy Street and find it was still possible to get interesting *hors d'œuvres* and kebab . . . to spend the night with other old friends, the Warbeys, near Kensington Gardens, and to be drawn, if only for those few hours, into their circle – a diverse group that evening, including a British Intelligence officer, a Russian and two naturalised Germans. . . . It was a world away from the somewhat limited conversation of George and Jenky.

Bill Warbey, with whom in the remote days of 1931 I had made pacifist speeches and demonstrations, was a press officer to the Norwegian Government exiled in London. I could only admire the confidence with which he had taken on the job, seeing that (to the best of my knowledge) he had never set foot in Norway or worked in Fleet Street. That, I realised, was the difference in our natures. In the field of writing I was always ready to have a go at anything, even when, like radio or television, it demanded special techniques I had to teach myself from scratch. In other ways I was too diffident, and would miss opportunities through a reluctance to risk failure. Bill Warbey was less apprehensive. In 1945 he sailed into Parliament on the crest of the Labour wave, and with one short break remained there until his retirement in 1966, as formidable a critic of his own leaders as of the Tories opposite.

Refreshed by this glimpse of a livelier world, I returned to my gritty hut in the Coventry fog and my dogged pedalling from one forlorn encampment to another. It was not easy to persuade myself that I was achieving much. Some detachments, with virtually nothing to do, seemed to welcome my visits. With others it was a constant struggle to get hold of the men for an hour. If an individual sought my help, he was almost invariably posted elsewhere.

On leave in Nottingham I contrived an encounter with the educational staff officer at the headquarters there, which were within ten minutes' walk of our house. He was the formidable Major Wigg, later famous as a Labour minister and a controversial life peer, and even then a legend for ruthless efficiency coupled with intense loyalty to his A.E.C. subordinates. A transfer, even to the remotest corner of his district, would be a good move, putting me under an exceptional chief and also bringing me closer to my family. Wigg later wrote that he would like to have me but it would depend on one of his

own sergeants wishing to make the exchange. I was not surprised when none of them wanted to leave him.

That April, however, I was given a move inside my own
district. I was sent to the 30th Warwickshires, a very similar
battalion, but concentrated at Packington Park, between Coventry and Birmingham.

Even army huts, latrines and 'ablutions' could not destroy
the beauty of that setting. It was high ground, airy, with smoke-
blue distances. I jotted down first impressions – I was finding
time and heart to use my notebook again:

A strip of the old Forest of Arden, with ancient oaks, many
dead, rotten and hollow; bracken; wild daffodils in two
fields at the foot of the hill; deer, small and dark-brown;
black-and-white Friesian cows, pigs, partridges, pheasants,
wood-pigeons . . . fish in the lake. Log fires.

There were in fact two lakes. The estate covered thousands
of acres. The Earl of Aylesford lived in the 'new' Hall, a classical
mansion that had stood there a mere century or two. The Old
Hall stood some distance away across the rolling parkland, and
served as battalion headquarters. I was given a desk in the main
office under the close and suspicious scrutiny of the R.S.M.

Once more the 'bleeding Sergeant' wished on the unit by the
A.E.C. had somehow to justify his existence. I busied myself as
best I could, moving round the park and making myself known
to the various company commanders, respectfully pressing for
a minimum of two periods a week for every man, whether I
took it myself or not. There was supposed to be a Current
Affairs session, based on the Army Bureau's weekly pamphlet,
which was more or less expert briefing on some topical subject,
Stalingrad or the Western Desert or the neutrality of Turkey.
We tried also to get a second period for more connected series
of discussions on the workings of parliamentary democracy,
local government, the law courts, the freedom of the press, and
so forth. For this we had the very clear and objective *British
Way and Purpose* pamphlets.

It was easy to make fun of these discussions, easy for remote,
eminent enthusiasts to exaggerate their value, but no less easy

for their prejudiced opponents to underestimate their ultimate effects. A. D. Lindsay had just written in the *Times Educational Supplement*:

> These men wanted to argue and discuss, and they were being encouraged to do so. There was almost universal testimony that discussion was free, and felt to be free. . . . I got the impression that there had not been an Army in England which discussed like this one since that famous Puritan Army which produced the Putney Debates and laid the foundation of modern democracy.

My own impression squared with Lindsay's. And it is now generally recognised that the army vote in the 1945 election, which swept Labour into power, was a good deal influenced by those preceding years of discussion.

This is not to suggest that the discussion-leaders exercised a political bias. It is true that in the A.E.C. itself there were probably more Socialists than Conservatives – at least that is suggested by those members of the Corps who stood for Parliament in 1945, and the M.P.s who leap first to mind are men like Wigg and Arthur Blenkinsop. But the A.E.C. was too thin on the ground to lead all the discussions itself, and most were taken by regimental officers representing a much wider cross-section. Also, there was throughout a strong emphasis on objectivity.

In my own experience with those two rather low-grade battalions I found a fair amount of invincible ignorance and prejudice. Often, with a secret inward chuckle, as I remembered my own tub-thumping past, I found myself quietly putting a Tory point of view. What else could one do, confronted with a platoon of thirty men, of whom half were politically illiterate and indifferent, half emotionally if not intellectually 'Labour', and not a single man capable of advancing a contrary opinion?

How much the men learned from these sessions I would not like to say. I myself learned a lot. Already, as a writer, I had moved far from my original propagandist position. In those army years I was forced to cultivate objectivity, but I soon came to love it for its own sake. My historical fiction, in particular, was never the same again.

Apart from these discussions – often conducted as we sprawled in the dry bracken, under the Arden oaks, in what I remember as one of the rather fine war-time summers – I did what else I could do to make up an educational programme. We had visiting civilian lecturers on popular science, and, remembering old Major Insh at Wakefield, and his enthusiasm for regional studies, I read up the historical and literary associations of the neighbourhood and talked about them. It was uphill work but not entirely wasted.

When all was said and done, however, I had not enough work. I spent hours at my table in the orderly room, and since I could not go on forever preparing talks and typing reports, I kept the keys clicking in other ways. I had a capacity for concentration in those days that now seems to me incredible. Despite the chatter going on around me, the constant buzzing of the switchboard, and the disapproving eyes of the R.S.M. boring into the close-cropped nape of my neck, I managed in those months to write a complete book, *Black Night, Red Morning*, which Blackwell published in the following year. This was a highly topical thriller set on the Russian Front, utilising my first-hand knowledge of Moscow and the Crimea. The climax was laid in Yalta, a place few English people had then heard of, two years before Churchill's conference with Stalin and Roosevelt, but one vivid in my own mind's eye from the sun-drenched weeks Marian and I had spent there in 1935.

I was strongly tempted to add a sly dedication, 'To the Officer Commanding, 30th Bn. The Royal Warwickshire Regiment, without whose lack of co-operation this story could never have been written'. Perhaps I did him an injustice. He may have believed in Army Education but been genuinely unable to provide more scope for my energies. I have my doubts.

At Packington I lived in a proper sergeants' mess. Only one character compared in human interest with the bibulous Jenky and the pawky George I had left behind (in soak, probably) at Coventry. This sergeant was in civil life a local carpenter. He had done a good deal of restoration work on Tudor cottages round Stratford-upon-Avon, and was much amused by the middle-class obsession with old beams, especially previously hidden ones revealed by the workmen. 'I always says,' he told me with a wink, 'if it's old beams they wants me to find – an' provided the money's all right – old beams they shall have. Even if I has to put 'em in when they're not lookin'.' He told tales of deer-poaching with the trip-wires that would have fitted smoothly into the Shakespeare legend, but in fact belonged to the current era of meat-rationing.

This character apart, the sergeants' mess at Packington survives in my mind only as a blurred picture of drowsy figures dozing after midday dinner in a tobacco-laden fog, through which ruminant voices penetrate my ears with fresh colloquial idioms for my notice, too many of them being picturesque synonyms for sexual congress and thus of no practical use to a writer of children's books.

This vagueness owes something to the isolation of the place and the good weather, which prompted me to vanish after tea, or even without waiting for it. Much as I had grumbled at Coventry, it had at least films, occasional plays, a bookshop and the chance to eat something, however unexciting, that had not come out of an army cookhouse. I had my bicycle, or there were double-decker buses passing the lodge-gates at the bottom of the hill. If the buses were full and did not stop, it was easy for a man in uniform to hitch a lift. I would come back late, finish the evening with tea and marmalade sandwiches at a lorry-drivers' café near the lodge, and make my way up to the sleeping camp through a darkness alive with rustling bracken and drifting deer.

So summer passed into autumn. I was spared the less idyllic experience of a winter in that vestigial corner of Arden. In January the warrant-officer running the district education office went off to take a commission. The major decided that I should replace him. So, without any demonstrations of grief on either side, I packed my kit and forsook the society of the Royal Warwicks for that of Royal Leamington Spa.

ONE great attraction of the move was the lack of space for me in the sergeants' mess at District Headquarters. I was thus permitted to take over my predecessor's comfortable civilian billet at the lower end of the town and once more enjoy the luxury of a bedroom, though a tiny one, to myself. It was a pleasant walk to the office, either up the urbane Victorian Parade or across the Jephson Gardens bordering the river.

My landlady was one of those decent working-class widows whose features, their natural bone-structure further sharpened by a lifetime of toil and anxiety, give little clue to the good nature and generosity within. Her youngest child, whose room I had, had followed his dead father into the Navy. The other three were girls. Doris, dark, austere of hair-style, fond of playing the 'Moonlight Sonata', worked in a greengrocer's, was married, but remained at her mother's while her husband was on active service. Frances I thought radiantly beautiful but unspoilt by vanity. She spoke little but brightened the meal-table as pure decoration. She worked in a factory. Lil worked in another. Lil, also good-looking in her way, was wide of mouth and hip, quick of tongue and temper, flinging in and out of the little house with boyish violence. We often sparred, and Mam would rebuke her in shocked tones, while I laughed. I think Mam sensed, as I did, that behind the joking lay a resentment against my involuntary presence in their home. It was natural enough, but the others never betrayed it.

Leam Street showed me a life I should never otherwise have known. I was treated as one of the family. I shaved over the scullery sink while Mam dodged behind me, frizzling breakfast. I waited discreetly for my turn before crossing the back-yard. Only the zinc bath-tub did I not share, preferring to use the Pump Room or the Toc H hostel.

I did share, with family, neighbours, relatives and chance callers, the cosy gossip of the living-room and the bright fire blazing in the range behind its tall fender. We sat close and companionable under the gaslight with its dangling chain. Somehow the small room accommodated not only the table and chairs but a settee, two armchairs, and a piano. There was a canary in a cage, a radio and a pendulum clock with a loud tick. The mantel was lined with photographs in fretwork frames, along with a pottery Sealyham and a Toby jug with Churchill's face.

I ate amply for my modest billeting allowance. A good breakfast, a hot midday dinner, a high tea, a bedtime snack of bread and cheese and pickles and cocoa. I was in clover. Only one thing irked me. With the front parlour unused, hushed and chilly, and no space to work in my narrow bedroom, there was nowhere to type without disturbing others.

Having managed, with relative ease, to get a whole book written at Packington Park, I had been encouraged to hope that things would be even better now, since, even if my days were more fully occupied and supervised, there would be the evenings. The changed mood of the war was a further encouragement. The Russians had won their crushing victory at Stalingrad, the enemy were beaten in north Africa, America was coming to the rescue. . . . One had only to stroll up the Parade in Leamington to notice the ever-growing numbers of American troops. The apocalyptic gloom of 1939 had changed by 1943 to the certainty of eventual victory. With reasonable luck I should survive the war and resume my free-lance writing career.

I had two very different projects I was keen to work upon. One was a third novel, more serious than the two light-weight satires I had already published, and perhaps unduly autobiographical. The second, which I had started in odd moments even during those strenuous months as an infantry private, was to be an anthology of Greek literature in the best available translations. It seemed a good idea at the time and a relatively novel one. It was not until 1955 that James and Janet Maclean

Todd did something of the kind, with Maurice Bowra's blessing, in *Voices from the Past*. Equally in the future, unknown to me, lay the great Penguin scheme for the publication of ancient classics in readable new translations, the success of which indicates that I was groping along the right lines. In the end I had to find quite a different way to transmit my enthusiasms to readers who had no Latin or Greek, by writing stories like *The Crown of Violet* and *Word to Caesar*.

At Leamington I found myself frustrated by my dependence on my typewriter. Since my first boyhood machine, I had let it become my master. Just as other people could make their first draft only by hand, I found pen or pencil tedious. I liked to know how a book was working out, how many thousand words were done and still to do, how much space had been used or could be spared for a particular passage. I liked to see the dialogue set out on the page, clear as print, and observe whether the paragraphs were running on too long. Silent scribbling was not for me. So to compose anything now, during my free evenings, became almost impossible. I struggled on with both books, but in the end neither came to anything, even with the occasional hour I could steal unnoticed at the office.

Headquarters occupied several big houses in Kenilworth Road. In one, seldom seen, was the major-general. Dispatch-riders chugged and snorted in and out of drive-gates, bearing brown envelopes to assorted units all over the West Midlands. Staff officers bustled between the once-desirable residences. A.T.S. clerks tripped to and fro, clutching manilla files to bosoms not enhanced by the flapped pockets of thick khaki tunics.

One such girl was our own Private Bissell, a dark-haired, downright-spoken Cockney, robust of form and character. If I ever knew her Christian name, I was not encouraged to use it. I fancy it was something incongruously soft and sweet, like Rosemary. So far as the Education Office was concerned, she was Bissell.

She and I worked in a small room at the rear of one house. A few more stairs led up to the first-floor front, where the afternoon sunshine streamed generously upon our superiors at their desks.

A new staff officer arrived about the same time as I did. Irish, dapper, though a little wild of hair and fey in manner, having Charles as a first name, he was inevitably nicknamed 'Champagne Charlie'. It was said that he had once been thrown from a horse and remained unconscious for three weeks. Cynics occasionally asked, 'When will the three weeks be up?'

He was excessively conscientious. As there was a war on, even the Education Office in Leamington must be ever vigilant and work seven days a week. Only once did we leave the telephone unmanned during the day. One Sunday afternoon, when he and I were holding the fort, he burst in exuberantly with two tickets for *Messiah* at a church just down the road. Would I care to go with him? I did. If any other trumpet sounded that afternoon, it met with no response from our department.

To Bissell and myself his most infuriating habit was mislaying files. We kept them all laid out, tagged and minuted, in our own room. I had scarcely seen a file in my life before, much less been taught to keep one, but I picked up invaluable hints which I later carried into civilian life, sometimes dumbfounding publishers who supposed authors to be incapable of system.

Late one afternoon, when Bissell had already left, the major's bell rang. I answered with misgivings. I had a forty-eight-hour pass in my pocket and must soon start for the train if I was to reach Nottingham that night.

The major wanted a file. I ran downstairs again. I might have known it. That file was nowhere to be seen. I raced back.

'You had it yesterday, sir. I remember Bissell – '

'She must have taken it back.'

'I think, sir – '

'She must have done.' He indicated his empty Out tray. And the file was not on his desk.

Feverishly I searched both rooms. Our sparse army furnishings made that easy. The minutes ticked by. Unaware of my personal preoccupation, the major grew agitated on his own account. The file, though concerned with some trivial matter, must be found if we stayed there all night.

There was one place I could not search. I had no key to the so-called Secret drawer, the very ordinary drawer in the major's desk that contained such documents as must, by regulation, be kept locked up. I asked him to open it.

'But that's ridiculous, Trease! Why on earth should I put a file like that in the Secret drawer?'

'I don't know, sir. But perhaps – '

'It's unthinkable. I am most meticulous about what goes into that drawer. Meticulous. There is nothing secret about the file; it would be absurd. You must have it downstairs. No doubt Bissell – '

I was already halfway down the stairs. But I knew a second search was pointless. Bissell was a girl who knew her job. I was going to miss that train to Birmingham, and the next one would be too late for a connection to Nottingham. I charged up to the major's office again and stood over him, hands clenching and unclenching in impotent fury, striving to keep a respectful poker-face though it was red and sweating.

'If you would just check the *Secret* drawer, sir – '

'Very well,' he said stiffly. He fumbled in his pocket and fished out his keys. 'Quite unaccountable,' he muttered as the drawer slid open to reveal the file. I murmured a well-controlled farewell and fled before he could think of anything else. Thanks to my cross-country running with the King's Own, I caught my train with a few seconds to spare.

The major was assisted by Captain Dummer and Lieutenant Stone, both regulars like himself. Dummer was very tall, gentle, rather solemn, a pre-war sergeant, an army schoolmaster of the old breed, experienced in teaching the three Rs and British Empire history to bandboys and garrison children in places like Gibraltar. The sort of education they were now organising was as fresh to these veterans as it was to us newcomers, and, since it took them into unfamiliar territory, cultural and potentially political, it sometimes filled them with alarm. Nothing, however, would have alarmed Stone. He was a little man, Dummer's complete opposite, and had once been a corporal in the Signals. Wanting a change, he told me, he had chosen the A.E.C. because, unlike some other arms of the service, it was content with a 'good' conduct record and did not insist on its being 'exemplary'.

Such was the triumvirate ruling my new life. I was now

promoted Warrant-Officer Class Two and exchanged my stripes for a laurel-encircled crown. It amused me to reflect that I had reached the same rank as I had held as Company Sergeant-Major of the school cadets. I was 'sir' to lower ranks, '*Mr* Trease' to my superiors. The 'Mr' had a sweet sound, recalling the lost civilian status that might one day be regained. It was suggested that I might like my name to go forward for an A.E.C. commission, but I knew that, as a junior officer, I should be even more involved in bureaucratic administration and have little or no lecturing and discussion-group work. I should lose much of the personal freedom I enjoyed, I should be thrust into the conventional atmosphere of an officers' mess, and, most certain of all, I should be posted away from the relatively pleasant ambience of Leamington Spa, never to return. Junior officers seemed to be for ever on the move. There was much to be said for staying where I was, observing life without too great a burden of responsibility.

On the last day of some financial period the office was plunged into crisis. The triumvirs had discovered belatedly that there was an allocation of a hundred pounds for cultural equipment which, if not spent by midnight that day, would vanish like Cinderella's coach.

I could not at first understand their dismay. If we had managed without the money until now, why not save it for the taxpayer? This heresy shocked them. I was instructed in one of the first maxims of bureaucracy: one must spend one's allocation, whether needed or not, or it may not be forthcoming in the future when it is. If I was to learn little about war in the Army, I was to learn much about bureaucracy.

The major was adamant. This money must be got rid of. But how? To spend a hundred pounds on culture, just like that, presented us with a baffling emergency.

I suggested that we divide the sum between gramophone records and prints, both to be lent out to units by the dozen or so A.E.C. instructors we had scattered throughout the District. This suggestion was eagerly clutched at. I was told to get on with it. I spent the rest of that morning in a music-shop on the Parade, listening to classical records. Then I took a train to Birmingham, found a couple of art shops with a fair stock of reproductions, and bought what would now seem, for fifty pounds, a remarkable number of pictures, ranging from the Impressionists to Rowland Hilder and Peter Scott, whose work was particularly in demand for the A.T.S. billets. My purchases, when displayed in the office, were endorsed with some slight misgivings. Stone, viewing probably for the first time the colourful Tahitians of Gauguin, observed darkly that he had seen girls like that in Alexandria and kept clear of them. Dummer, mainly concerned that the expenditure could be justified to higher authority, remarked thankfully that we were 'covered'. A natural Civil Servant in khaki, he liked at all times to be 'covered'. 'More than what *they* are,' said Stone.

Protocol was something I had never encountered in civilian life, so its military form struck me as a bizarre and absurd novelty. Bissell, of course, knew all about it and accepted it with a shrug of the shoulders and a toss of her coltish head. Men in khaki, she seemed to suggest, were as mad as, but no madder than, the rest of their sex. She was trained to know which letter must go out signed by the major in his own right, and which on behalf of the Command Education Officer or our own major-general. As they were all signed by the major, it did not seem to me important. Similarly, when cutting a stencil for some circular addressed to all the assorted units in the District, she could list them at the top of the letter in impeccable order of precedence. It was my misfortune that my ability to type had become known, so, when the invaluable Bissell was off-duty, what was more natural than to 'get Mr Trease to rattle it off'? People who cannot themselves type always imagine that, for those who can, even with two fingers, the process is practically instantaneous. Thus it was that one Sunday afternoon, when I had looked forward to a little undisturbed writing of my own, the major asked me to cut a stencil for some communication to a large selection of units. Had it been every unit in the area, I could have copied a standard list. Fatally, I had to compose it myself.

After a long time, for it was a tedious job, I went to him, feeling very self-righteous. He took one glance and the wild Irish hair stood on end.

'It can't go out like this!'

'Why not, sir?'

'You've put the Pioneers in front of the Royal Engineers. And – look – the Dental Corps! Right up *there!*' He snatched a pencil. He began ringing names and giving them arrows up and down the foolscap page. My neat list soon resembled a diagram of agitated spermatozoa.

I withdrew crestfallen. No literature was produced that afternoon.

If our activities at Leamington Spa seem now unforgivably frivolous in a war that was so full of heroism and horror, it is fair to remark that in those early months of 1944 few British soldiers were any more dramatically occupied. A minority were enduring tough campaigns in Italy or Burma, but even in this fifth year of the struggle most had seen no more Germans or Japanese, fired no more shots, than I had. Along with an ever-mounting number of Americans and Canadians, together with the exiled forces of occupied Europe, they were still waiting for the opening of that 'Second Front' demanded by Communist slogan-daubers on every available wall.

The brunt of the land war was borne by the Russians. It was considered important that our troops should know more about their allies on the Eastern Front, and this gave me a chance to escape from the office. My first-hand knowledge of Russia became more than ever an asset. A trial lecture was arranged and the general himself came to vet me.

After the first minutes I forgot the brasshats in the front row. I had given the talk so often, I knew what interested most people and what made them laugh. I knew the regular questions, including the traps, and I had answers.

When it was over, the general tackled me. Hadn't I felt, travelling through Russia, that I was living in a police state? I told him honestly that, though I had known it to be so, I had never felt personally restricted. My wife and I had walked for miles, not only in the streets of Moscow, Leningrad and other towns, but in the wooded hills above Yalta, and it had been inconceivable that we should be under continuous surveillance. Of course there had been places barred to us, but not places we had wanted to enter, anyhow, and wasn't that true even of Britain, especially Britain at war? Russia had been in something like a war situation ever since the Revolution. . . . He grunted and did not press his point. I wondered if, objective though I had tried to be, I had cooked my goose. But next day I was told his verdict: 'This man is to lecture as widely as possible in the District.'

Thereafter I enjoyed more freedom of movement and travelled all over Warwickshire, a region I had never known before the war. I was often in Kenilworth, off duty as well as on. I became familiar with the castle, which came in useful some years later when I needed it as a setting for several essential episodes in my story of Simon de Montfort, *The Barons' Hostage*. Over the years I was acquiring a greater and greater reluctance to lay scenes against real backgrounds of which I had no first-hand knowledge. Even Birmingham had been until then an unknown city, and I felt a rush of embarrassment when I saw the Bull Ring as it was then. Ten years earlier, in *Comrades for the Charter*, I had described the street battles there in the summer of 1839, but, though I had worked conscientiously from the news-paper descriptions of the time, I had never realised that the area had been not flat but on a steepish hill. I knew what a difference it might have made to the whole feeling of the affair and I wondered if I had unwittingly written nonsense. I was relieved when I was able to get hold of a copy and see that I had said nothing inconsistent with the facts, and, when I revised the story for a new edition many years later, there seemed no need to do more than slip in the single word 'sloping'. But that discovery taught me a lesson. I developed the habit of recording places even though I had no plan to use them as backgrounds, and over and over again I found the notes valuable at some later date.

One of my regular ports of call in Birmingham was Sir Oliver Lodge's old home in Edgbaston, then occupied by the Military Police. If I had a week-end pass to Nottingham, it was convenient to complete my day's work there, so that I was already halfway home. Dummer was most co-operative. He would ring the Military Police and offer my services for Friday afternoon. No, I would hear him tell them regretfully, no other day or time was possible. Mr Trease was in great demand.

Dummer was a kindly fellow, and, so far as rank allowed, we became good friends, though he never used my Christian name until after he had ceased to be my superior. I saw more of him than the others, for our office was reduced to sub-district status and only we two remained, sharing one room. When he went into hospital for an operation I had to run the office alone and prepare the quarterly report for some high-level signature. I remembered Dummer's nervous refrain, 'So long as we're *covered*', and concocted a favourable account of our activities which nobody would know enough to contradict. The more difficult thing was to bring myself to write in clichés and official jargon, but I knew from experience that any phrasing which still showed the merest nervous twitch of life would be instantly trodden on by some bureaucratic boot.

I studied the previous quarterly report we had prepared together. We had totalled the figures as impressively as we could, adding up the fortnightly returns made by all our A.E.C. instructors. Lectures were classified according to audience, 'men', 'women' or 'mixed'. Dummer would frown at the statistics, eager to improve them but determined to be covered. A thought would seize him.

'That talk you gave at Warwick! There were some A.T.S. as well as the Ordnance chaps?'

'Yes, sir – '

'Suppose we counted it *here*, under "Men" – and it would be quite fair to include it again, under "Women" – '

'*And* "Mixed",' I said encouragingly.

The total rose by two. These pettifogging methods, however, made me impatient. 'Look, sir,' I said, 'one thing is certain, isn't it? The figures *must* always go up on the last quarter?'

'Ye-es.' He hesitated, but I knew there was no doubt in his mind.

'Right, sir. Then why not decide on a suitable total to begin with, and then make the others add up to it? We'll have to do that in the end, so why waste time fiddling about with ones and twos?'

'But – we must be covered.'

Cover could always be found. I just resented the time wasted in finding it.

Dummer went with me to some of my lectures. It gave him a chance to get round the units and eased my transport problem, since he could ask for a car and driver, but I could not.

For evening meetings in A.T.S. billets I prepared a light talk on Russian life with such special feminine interest as I could devise. Dummer would solemnly introduce me, stressing that here was a speaker who had actually lived and worked in that unfamiliar land. I can see him now, on one unforgettable occasion, rising to his considerable height, then leaning forward across the table, and fixing the girls with so earnest a gaze that, for a moment at least, they paused in their knitting.

'Mr Trease is going to speak to us tonight about. . . . ' He too paused. ' "Women in the Soviet Union".' He went on with ponderous emphasis, 'And I may say Mr Trease speaks *from first-hand experience!*' There was a roar of earthy appreciation from that extremely hard-boiled roomful of drivers, cooks and orderlies. After such an introduction nothing I could say came as anything but an anticlimax.

So the spring passed into that beautiful early summer of 1944. Marian and Jocelyn came down for a day or two. There was no room for us all at Leam Street, but with some difficulty I found accommodation in a guest-house. We strolled in the grounds of Warwick Castle, saw the peacocks spread their tails, and asked a friendly stranger to photograph us together against the battlements. Every soldier needed family snapshots in his wallet. They were the great social solvent in all those chance encounters that did something to mitigate the loneliness of separation from all that really mattered. With acquaintances of the opposite sex they served as an indication, if not an absolute guarantee, of innocent intentions. I must have displayed these particular photographs to the civilian typist who had taken the place of the departed Bissell, for I reported rather proudly to Marian that Jane had taken them off to show to her colleagues in the typing-pool.

Apparently the effect of you in your slacks, leaning against a bit of Warwick Castle as though you owned the whole place, was terrific! 'Isn't she smart?' and 'She's *terribly* sophisticated, isn't she?' were comments made, apparently in tones of awe and envy. So now you know. . . . Today I'm madly busy – I had two talks this morning, I have a play-reading tonight, and a pile of routine matters this afternoon. So this letter must be short.

At any time, now, routine was liable to abrupt termination. Several of our A.E.C. instructors had been posted off to 21 Army Group, ready for the invasion of Europe. Their probable role would be to run the front-line newspapers, so valuable for keeping up morale, as the *Tobruk Truth* and *Eighth Army News* had demonstrated during the African fighting. I never knew when I might be sent off to a similar assignment. All leave had been stopped – that was why Marian had had to come to Leamington. On 4 June, just two days before D-Day, had I but known, I was writing in my notebook:

Still, still awaiting the Second Front – or, as we now call it, the invasion. (Funny, to think of *our* side invading any one else. The word rings oddly.)
Shall we remember in years to come, when these historic weeks are dramatised, that in spite of all the mounting preparations and suspense we went on seeing Shakespeare at Stratford and Pirandello in Birmingham, that we walked and cycled, dined out, had tea in half-timbered inns and trod softly in the Beauchamp Chapel at St Mary's, Warwick . . . that Jocelyn paddled and swung, on her week-end visit . . . that we all planned for the future and talked eagerly of 'after the war' – where we'd live, and travel, what we'd eat and wear and buy. There was so little reminder of the war except the planes throbbing overhead at night, 'softening up', bombing the French railway junctions; the white stars appearing on Army vehicles, the red shield and blue cross appearing on more and more khaki shoulders; leave stopped, trains cut, occasional tank columns rumbling south. . . .
And still the Leam cool and green in its shadows, the Avon fair and blue under the theatre terraces . . . the pink chestnuts ranged massive round the Pump Room gardens, or standing, lone, in a field of young corn . . . Hampton Lucy church tower slender above the trees, and languid cattle deep

in buttercup meadows . . . a proud young gipsy on a high-standing piebald horse . . . and Henry Wood's jubilee Prom in London on the 10th.

The next entry is headed 'Guy's Cliff, June 6th, 4.30 p.m.'

And this morning it came. . . . Most people were disturbed by the extra-heavy air traffic during the night – I slept through it myself, though. 8 a.m. radio brought rumours – German reports. Just after 9.30, hastily gathering round the radio, we heard the official communique, the repeated warnings in English, French, Flemish, Dutch, Norwegian, Danish . . . and then the quiet American tones of Eisenhower, followed by King Haakon and the other national leaders.

We all stood round very intent, rather conscious, I think, that we were living through a 'historic moment'. I thought of that Sunday morning, September 3rd, 1939, when we'd sat by the radio at Abingdon. I felt a great lightening of the heart. The five-year frost of life is breaking. Whatever lies ahead, it's spring now.

It's been a day of sun and shower. I write this on a bench by the old Saxon mill, with the broad pool of the Avon, reedy, water-lilied, and a little frothy, spreading away at my feet towards the big house.

'The big house' was that romantic, crag-perched mansion to which Sarah Kemble was bundled off by her parents in 1771 in their ineffectual attempt, by turning her into a lady's companion, to protect her from the advances of William Siddons. This was yet another scene that I took note of, from professional habit, without any notion that I should need it twenty years later when I included Sarah Siddons in a book of short theatrical biographies which I called *Seven Stages*.

On D-Day I was not thinking of her. I sat on the bench and wrote in my notebook: 'A hen picks at the earth. Unseen aircraft throb. Birds twitter. And not even in the streets of Leamington and Warwick was there the slightest sign of "history at work".' Which, in itself, was a salutary lesson for a writer of historical fiction.

THE Normandy landings brought no dramatic change to my routine. I noticed one difference. I was personally responsible for several military hospitals, mostly in country mansions secluded among the Warwickshire lanes. These hospitals began to fill. For the men who were not too badly wounded I had to arrange talks, discussions, quizzes, gramophone recitals, even spelling bees. One or two, incapacitated but mentally alert, wanted to start correspondence courses, sometimes on highly technical subjects. What I noticed was the superior average intelligence of these hospital patients, compared with that of the troops I had previously met. The units I had been dealing with had included a large proportion of men with low medical grades, and I now realised what cynical old hands had meant by the 'category mentality'. There really was a relationship between physical fitness and intellectual response. The A1 fighting soldier still displayed it, retaining the mental qualities even after he had been badly wounded.

It was worth making a big effort to help these keen individuals, if only by getting them the information, pamphlets, application-forms and books they needed. I used to cycle off with a packed saddle-bag and a book-filled grip slung on my handlebars. There was some ribaldry from the other officers at Headquarters. 'Nurse Trease out on another case,' they said.

Frustratingly, I was never sure that I should see a particular patient again. He might be transferred to another hospital or convalescent home, returned to depot, or invalided home, and there was no chance to follow up. As men disappeared, so did library books. They had always been a problem, with units of any kind. They came in boxes from the public library, which did not take kindly to a wastage of twenty or thirty per cent.

Dummer came in one day after a gruelling interview with the county librarian. He looked like a very large, very gentle dog that had been unjustly whipped. 'But I *told* her,' he wailed, 'she has only to claim on the proper form – the War Office will pay.'

'And what did she say, sir?'

'She said she didn't want money, she wanted her books.'

I tried to explain that most books were now virtually irreplaceable. Production was down through material shortages, consumption was up because the mass of the population was reading as never before. Reading was one of the few activities that war conditions actually favoured. People could read to while away the tedium of long hours on duty. In air-raid shelters, First Aid posts, barrack-rooms and trains, on fire-watching spells and silent switchboards – in a hundred situations unbookish people were discovering the incomparable convenience and solace of the printed word. The print order of a new book was conditioned mainly by the publisher's supply of paper. I think Blackwell printed ten thousand copies of *Black Night, Red Morning* and told me that they could easily have sold them (as some publishers did) in advance of publication-day. They themselves preferred to keep a title in print as long as they could, rationing the booksellers to so many copies at a time. Selling was so easy, so automatic, that the author could take no pride in his figures, and I used to look forward to a day when competition would return and royalty-statements regain their sporting interest.

We tried hard to impress on units that they were answerable for the books we took them. They must keep a proper check. If a man was posted away, his books must not vanish with him.

This appeal was taken to heart. One sergeant-major was over-zealous. He led us proudly into Company Office and pointed his cane at a familiar-looking box under his table. 'There you are, sir, all present and correct! No need to check 'em. Box hasn't been unlocked since I signed for it.'

The books had been there for three months. But he was 'covered' and so, I suppose, were we. Somewhere, in one of our reports, it could be truthfully recorded that another fifty volumes had been supplied for the use of the troops.

I myself continued to be an avid library-user all the time I was in Leamington. Were we, so many millions of us, in those abnormal war-time conditions, the last generation of really hungry readers? There was no television. Many of us had no opportunity for private, selective radio-listening. We were lonely, exiled and deprived.

Those who, like me, had an easy war do not like to make a song about our trivial experiences. Compared with those of the battle-front – not to mention the prison-camp – they offer cause for thankfulness rather than complaint. Yet by the standards of normal existence, as taken for granted by subsequent generations, they amounted to something. 'The mere deprivation of liberty', humane penologists frequently remind us, 'is sufficient punishment.' And, though we were not behind bars, we were essentially 'deprived of liberty' for periods of up to six years. Tell a modern young man, or his wife, that for six years they will be separated, lucky if they can meet at intervals for a week-end or a few days – and that even the wife is not going to be living in their former home. If it is a job you are offering, it will need to be well paid. Yet (as in my own case and Marian's) these were the common circumstances of even an 'easy war'.

So . . . one read.

Dear Leamington Library, what did I *not* read? I kept no record. I read, as always, a lot of unmemorable light novels. I believe that even the venerable Marx did the same. My note-book mentions only a few books that seemed worthy of comment. Van Gogh's letters, Ostrovsky's *Even the Wise Man Stumbles*, Balzac, Stendhal . . . I was trying to fill some of the gaps left by my too narrowly classical education. I was conscious too that, by abandoning Oxford, I had missed the intellectual discipline I recognised and envied in university graduates, or at least the best of them. In the past two or three years I had subjected myself to a good deal of painful self-examination.

For several reasons this was a period of deep unhappiness, though I did not commit much of it to my notebook, which remained chiefly a writer's storehouse of observations. I used it for scraps of authentic dialogue overheard, like the murmured gossip of two usherettes in the dark cinema gangway: 'After all *she's* bin through? You ask me to believe they slept in separate rooms?' Or an evocative glimpse of a character, a beautiful unknown girl on a passing bus or a mahogany-faced bargee gliding beneath a canal bridge. Or a Warwickshire landscape, a weather effect, or a still-life impression: 'Creamy-white tulips in a Leamington florist's . . . the petals bright-white where they caught the light, and soft shadows of palest yellow like curds. I saw them, in my mind's eye, in a plain black jug against an egg-green wall.' The jug was one we had bought in our first married days in Bath. The wall was that of our living-room at Abingdon.

Another reason for my dejected mood was a new pessimism about my future as a writer. I had changed my billet and now lodged with a family much closer to Headquarters. Here it was understood that I could have a room to myself when I wanted to type, and this was the reason I offered at Leam Street, with some awkwardness and guilt, when I broke the news of my departure. Mam and her daughters had been kind and long-suffering. It was impossible to leave their house without hurting their feelings. Lil eyed me with suppressed hatred and did not trust herself to speak. She could not understand a writer's irrational hunger for privacy.

My new landlady, Mrs Oscroft, understood. She had two bright schoolgirl daughters and they found it interesting to have a children's author in the house. The girls generously offered to lend me their comics, and were surprised, though not offended, when I explained that they were not my normal reading. 'We send all our comics out to Daddy,' they explained, 'and he says that all the soldiers read them.' Daddy was a pharmacist in a military hospital in India.

Even in these more sympathetic surroundings my writing went badly. I could find no publisher for my anthology of extracts from Greek literature, on which I had spent a great deal of time, reading widely to find the best translations then available, choosing suitable passages to group together, and laboriously typing them out. When I finished my novel it was much longer and heavier than my two previous efforts, and the paper shortage gave Chapman & Hall an easy excuse for declining it. I had a gnawing fear that I had reached my limit with my children's books and those two light novels, and that

I had nothing further to offer. One way and another, my spirits were at their nadir. I felt again something like the dreadful gloom of adolescence, which had occasionally swept over me in the loneliness of Gosforth and now flooded back like a black tide.

Life, of course, had its brighter side.

That D-Day summer I managed to see most of the Shakespeare productions at Stratford, and enjoyed them with an intensity I cannot recapture today when I see eccentric interpretations mounted with vastly more generous resources. Those Stratford evenings were unforgettable. Later, when I came to plan a documentary travel-story, *The Young Traveller in England and Wales*, taking a group of imaginary children on a tour that should show them all I considered most significant and attractive in the kingdom, I could think of no better climax than to end the tale on a September night in Stratford, the moon turning the Avon to silver, as the audience streamed out elated from a performance of the *Dream*. It was, as the girl in the book was made to say, 'just something I wanted specially to remember'.

There was a rail-car, old-fashioned even in 1944, that used to run down the local branch-line across the pastoral landscape of Shakespeare's childhood. Sometimes I reached Stratford in time for dinner at the Swan's Nest, a civilised meal in elegant surroundings, served with an awareness that everyone was theatre-bound, even the pink-cheeked Canadian air-pilots and their adoring companions. The real rush came – for me – at the end of the performance. I dared not miss that late rail-car lurching through the summer darkness back to Leamington, and sometimes I had to run half the way to the station. A splendid, spell-binding *Hamlet*, which went on a shade longer than usual, almost finished me as it decimated the Danish court. I caught the train and collapsed breathless. As I recovered by degrees, I listened to the conversation between an airman and a W.A.A.F. girl. They too had been at the play, but separately, and had left the theatre at different times in order to make sure of the train.

'I wonder,' said the girl wistfully, 'how it ended.'

'Dunno,' said the airman, 'but when *I* come away they were makin' a hole in the floor.'

Sad, I thought, that they had missed the climax, but much sadder that *Hamlet* was not much oftener acted to people with fresh minds, who did not know 'how it ended', and who did not feel bound to demonstrate their sophistication by comparing the performance with half a dozen previous interpretations. One of the stimulating experiences of those years was to study the reactions of ordinary men and women 'exposed to culture' (to adopt the horrid modern jargon) in a way they would not otherwise have been. I took a party of A.T.S. girls to *The Taming of the Shrew*, which was a foreseeable success, but more remarkable was the response to other Shakespearean plays by illiterates. We had in Warwickshire, at Wootton Wawen, a residential centre for illiterate soldiers which had become, under an inspired A.E.C. warrant officer instructor, a showplace that was the pride of the War Office. Adult illiteracy had been virtually unsuspected in Britain before the war, the Army had revealed it, and the A.E.C. had to cope, using Canadian textbooks at first because none existed in Britain. It was an intractable problem. Some of the men were, inevitably, of sub-normal type, but a number were quite intelligent and owed their illiteracy to childhood illnesses or the nomadic life of fairground families, bargees, and the like. I was always thankful that this kind of instruction never came my way – I should have been hopeless at the job – but I knew about Wootton Wawen because we administered it. I felt dubious when I first heard that parties were being taken to the Memorial Theatre. How, I wondered, would illiterates comprehend the richness of Shakespeare? I need not have worried. My colleague's instinct was sound. The theatre trips were a staggering success, and they paid dividends in the classroom afterwards.

That September I enjoyed another agreeable interlude.

Dummer sat frowning at a circular from Western Command. 'They want us to send someone on *this*,' he groaned – and I was instantly on my guard. Whatever 'this' was, it meant a disruption of somebody's placid existence and would probably be arduous and unpleasant. We had perhaps a dozen A.E.C. sergeants and warrant officers at our disposal, attached to units where in theory their presence was indispensable. My heart sank when Dummer went on, 'I was wondering about *you*.'

Luckily, before I could throw myself into an obstructive
posture, he passed me the circular.

It concerned a short course, Monday to Saturday, held at
regular intervals at Oxford. The original scheme had been to
offer Canadians on leave an authentic taste of life as lived in an
ancient English university. They would have rooms in Balliol,
attend a few lectures, dine in hall, and participate in a number
of typical activities. The idea had paid off. It had been extended
to Americans and other Allies. Now it was felt that the
atmosphere would be even more authentic with a leavening of
native British among the overseas visitors.

'Of course,' Dummer explained quickly, 'in your case you
would be there on duty. It wouldn't count as leave.'

I forced myself to point out that it seemed hardly fair for me
to enjoy this privilege. I had been at Oxford. Ought we not to
send someone who would get more out of it as a fresh experience? To my relief he brushed aside that argument. The
British were being sent not for their own sakes but to make the
course better for the others, who after all were paying with their
own money and attending in their own time. As an erstwhile
undergraduate, I should be peculiarly well qualified to make a
contribution.

I had often dreamed – literally, in my sleep – of a return to
Oxford to complete the business unfinished when I dropped out
in 1929. I still do sometimes, even now. Usually the dream,
whatever fantastic and incongruous form it assumes, lasts long
enough to reach the essential point of realisation that, for the
second time, I must throw up everything and go. It was strange
to walk into the porter's lodge, this time at Balliol, and re-enact
the formalities, see my name ticked on a list and be told the
number of my room and staircase. The resemblance ended
there. My waking week at Balliol was unalloyed pleasure,
undisturbed by any of the bogeys that beset my phantasmal
returns to Queen's.

There were some dozens of us on the course, Canadians,
Americans, a few Poles and British, drawn from all three armed
services and ranging from an American colonel to a Polish
woman corporal. Within the walls of Balliol all rank was
forgotten. We were there to enjoy ourselves. We British,

nominally on duty, had only a single instruction, to mix. It was easy to obey.

I struck up a particular friendship that week with Waverley Glover, a negro sergeant in the medical corps, from Mount Vernon, Ohio, a gentle, cultured, appreciative man whom I took to from our first encounter. He was describing his initial impressions of England after landing at Plymouth and seeing the rural landscape through the windows of the train. 'I thought of Wordsworth at once,' he said simply, 'and I felt at home.' That last word touched me, coming from a black American.

It was a joy to show him Oxford during our free time, especially the hidden corners he would scarcely have discovered by himself. 'That certainly is sump'n,' he would murmur reverently. Those words became a theme song. In hall we exchanged sixpenny coupons for half-pints of beer or cider, magnificently served in gleaming tankards. I remember once pointing out to him, and translating the Latin inscription to prove it, that he was imbibing his sixpenny-worth from a vessel presented to the College by 'James, Duke of Monmouth'. Waverley drained it with added zest and wiped his lips. 'That certainly is sump'n,' he said huskily. He was also much impressed by the generous provision of public lavatories in British towns, which he rightly felt to be the mark of high civilisation and correct priorities.

The week flew. We had our lectures, voluntary, of course, for that was the essence of Oxford, but well attended.

Rhodes House put on a reception and dance. Dons' wives and daughters were our hostesses. At the New Theatre we were taken to an all-star touring production of Congreve's *Love for Love*. On a third evening we were transported to North Oxford for one of those legendary musical evenings provided by Ernest Walker and the Misses Deneke.

There was by this date a distinct feeling that the end of the war, in Europe at least, was drawing near. London was suffering the new flying bombs, but in the rest of the country the tension had relaxed as the Allied armies pushed eastwards towards the Rhine. No one knew how long it would take to beat the Japanese, but it seemed improbable that everybody would be needed in the Far East. Hearts beat hopefully when the Government came out with its plans for a fair and orderly demobilisation to obviate the chaos that had followed the First World War. The soldier's age was balanced against the length of his service, a year of age (if I remember right) being equated with two months' service, so that a man who was six years younger than another, but had been called up into the Army twelve months earlier, was put into the same 'release group'. I came into Group 31. It was good to see the fact entered into my pay-book in November 1944, and to catch a glimpse of daylight at the end of the long tunnel.

Things went on at Leamington much the same. It seemed not unlikely that I should finish my military service there. The demobilisation period was going to be a busy time for the A.E.C. When the fighting stopped there would be millions of men with nothing much to do until their group came up for release. Many would require only to be kept interested and amused with popular talks, discussions, music recitals and so forth, but there would be a considerable minority anxious to better themselves. They would not all want to go back to the civilian job which, by law, their old employer had to offer them. There would be grants for university courses and emergency teacher-training colleges. Many men, in maturity, had discovered a vocation for teaching. And there would be all kinds of other schemes whereby ex-soldiers could be helped to qualify for new careers. Army Education had to prepare answers to many imminent questions. That autumn, like almost every other A.E.C. instructor, I went to one of a series of preparatory conferences in Lancashire.

Until Germany was beaten and this vast educational effort could begin, I continued my round of units in Warwickshire, talking on Russia and repeating my little essays into popular culture, 'A Play Is Born', 'Round Europe in Music' – a familiar classical record from each of ten countries – or a recital of West Midland poetry and prose, ranging from Michael Drayton to Housman and even Mary Webb.

One evening I was asked to give 'A Play Is Born' to a civilian society in Leamington. It went well. *After the Tempest* got the usual laughs, if not quite as lewd as those it drew from the rude soldiery. But I remember the occasion because afterwards I was led up for presentation to a regal figure who seemed to me, comparatively young as I was then, practically a historical relic. She was the widow of Sir George Alexander, stately, octogenarian, dressed to the nines in pink, with an enamelled face and an ornate walking-stick. She talked familiarly of Oscar Wilde, flattered me shamelessly by suggesting that some of my lines had reminded her of him, and reminisced about the Nineties as though they had been the day before yesterday. I enjoyed the flattery and the illusion of stepping back, for ten minutes, into a remote and mannered century.

Cultural talks and activities were in great demand for the A.T.S. companies thickly scattered through our area. The girls were less interested in Current Affairs lectures about remote war fronts or the political background of minor neutrals. I did more and more work with them in Leamington, Warwick, Stratford, Birmingham and elsewhere, and this did not diminish, but rather increased, when our department was reinforced by a woman subaltern, Mrs Norton, an impressive figure with her superbly cut, scarlet-lined greatcoat and monocle, and by one of the new A.T.S. sergeants who were now entering Education. Local history and citizenship came into our programme, and produced one or two memorable moments. I had tracked down, on a solitary walk, the wood near Warwick where a monument commemorates the savage liquidation of Edward II's favourite, Piers Gaveston, and one summer evening I conducted a large contingent of A.T.S. girls to view it. It was only as this seemingly endless file of khaki-clad girls threaded their way along a field-path and disappeared into the sombre thicket with me, a lone male figure, at their head, that I looked round and met the incredulous stare of a farm labourer, and realised that there might be something ambiguous in the spectacle. On another occasion I had to conduct a similar party to Warwick Assizes for a practical demonstration of British justice, and we had no sooner taken our places in the public gallery than the next case was called and the charge stated as indecent exposure. I went rather hot. Apart from anything else, it would be embarrassing if the judge looked up, noticed us, and made a pointed recommendation that we should withdraw. To my relief, and no doubt to the girls' disappointment, the prisoner at once pleaded guilty and no evidence had to be called.

Arts courses for the A.T.S. were now being run by Western Command at their Chester headquarters, and I was enlisted to make a fortnightly visit, taking two or three consecutive periods. These girls were voluntary applicants from all over the Command and were thus a particularly responsive audience. I gave them my well-tried favourite, 'A Play Is Born', but had to find something else as well. In recent years I had been growing fonder and fonder of Pepys. My introduction had been, long before, through Fagan's stage-play, *And So To Bed*. I had read the Diary at Gosforth and used Pepys as a character in one episode of *The Grey Adventurer*. I was developing an interest in him that would deepen with the years, so that by 1972 I could essay a biography for adults, *Samuel Pepys and His World*, and in 1973 a radio play and junior novel, *Popinjay Stairs*, in which he was a central figure. By 1944 I was sufficiently in love with the subject to adapt it for the Chester courses. I worked out a talk, with readings from the Diary, called 'Meet Mr Pepys'. It went down well. The Diary excerpts could hardly fail, including as they did poor Sam's timid and furtive flirtations, his marital troubles, and some of his other more comical misadventures. I could claim no scholarly knowledge of the period – my research into Pepysian London came decades later – but I had enthusiasm and I could tell that some of the audience had become infected with it. I like to think that there are a few dozen women alive today with a taste for Pepys which they first acquired during those hilarious sessions.

For me the Chester visits made a pleasant break. I slept the previous night at the Toc H hostel and had a free evening to explore the city. It always seemed to be fine. I never tired of strolling round those walls, whether at night or during my lunch-break the following day. I jotted down notes without any idea of how or when I should weave them into a book. Winter did not break the spell. I wrote in February:

Walking along the old city wall, among the roof-tops and upper storeys and back yards, now and then crossing some street, over a battlemented archway. Then, suddenly, the ramparted walk drops a little – the broad Dee is below, with its white weirs slanting noisily from bank to bank. . . . On the other side, muddy banks and upturned boats and a girl, glamorous by her remoteness, blonde, dark-slacked, red-jerseyed, moving beside her beached craft. Sea-gulls.

This scene, merely changed from a sunny winter noon to a September evening, appeared later in *The Young Traveller in England and Wales* like this:

From these Rows another flight of steps led to the walls, from which they could look down into busy streets, quiet private gardens, and warehouse-yards. . . . There was one grand stretch where the wall ran high above the River Dee, one of the greatest of the Welsh rivers, with a long salmon-weir slanting from bank to bank and the water tumbling and foaming over it. Sea-gulls wheeled overhead. Upturned boats lined the mudbanks opposite, two fishermen in gum-boots were patiently tinkering with a net, a girl in slacks was painting a dinghy bright blue . . . and the sun was going down in the west, lighting up one tangled cloud-mass and turning it into the fantastic likeness of a dragon, the red dragon that was the symbol of Wales.

I wonder who that girl was. She might have been surprised to learn that one day children would read about her in far-off places like Israel and Japan.

That April, 1945, Marian decided to go back to Abingdon. Our tenants were ready to leave. There was no need to stay with my mother, for the end of the war in Europe could not be far away, and the original reasons, air raids and evacuees and billeting, no longer applied. Jocelyn was seven and a half and was outgrowing the odd little private school round the corner which had sufficed until now. Marian, for her part, had endured almost four years of war-time existence in a big industrial city very different from any environment she had known before. And, though neither of us had much affection for Abingdon, where we had made only two or three close friendships and had met many a cold shoulder, one's own home was one's own home. Off and on we had discussed moving, but a return to Green Garth was the essential first step.

Here, however, we came up against the formidable bureaucracy created by the war. Was it because Abingdon lay south of the Thames in a zone still theoretically vulnerable to Nazi invasion? Whatever the reason, all accommodation was still controlled by a miniature dictator in the Council offices. To Marian's humble inquiry, 'If our tenants move out, may we have our own home again?' came the inflexible answer, 'Your request cannot be considered until the dwelling-house is vacant.' No advance arrangements were thus possible. Our local dictator might see fit to instal complete strangers. He would not say, one way or the other.

Marian was privately advised that a *fait accompli* was the best course. She and Jocelyn stayed the night with a friend close by. Then, with careful synchronisation and the connivance of our outgoing tenants, as they departed mother and child flung themselves desperately into their own home. A generation later, squatters would be taking over houses with infinitely more arrogance than a lawful owner dared display in 1945.

The local dictator accepted the situation. He may have realised that his days, like Hitler's, were numbered. Marian was permitted to remain.

VE-Day, 'Victory in Europe', came a few weeks later. Rather an anticlimax, I recorded in my notebook, after all we had been through since my entry on its first page. The news had been expected for so long. A general day off was announced as soon as I reached the office. Home was barely fifty miles away. I joined the exuberant khaki and blue-clad hitchhikers strung along the road that led out of town to Banbury and Oxford. Flags were coming out. Shrill self-conscious adolescents were capering round the Martyrs' Memorial. By midday I had reached the quiet haven of my own house and garden. A soft rain was falling through the sycamore branches, Haydn's London Symphony was coming from the radio. The war, the war against Hitler, at least, was over. At that moment nobody wanted to remember Japan.

When I lectured at Chester the following week I noticed that Colonel Clive-Webster, the Command Education Officer, was

sitting in the back row with a young A.T.S. junior-commander.
They came forward afterwards and made gratifying comments.
The young woman was on leave from Italy, a country I had
never seen. She described the work she was doing at a big
forces education centre that had been established at Perugia,
now that there was so much free time for such things, the
fighting done. Her enthusiasm kindled me. I found myself
saying:

'Would there be anything there, ma'am, for my kind of
thing?'

'But of *course*, Mr Trease! If you'd be interested – '

'None of that, now,' the colonel interrupted good-
humouredly. 'You're not having him.'

So my long love-affair with Italy was destined to be put off
for a whole decade. Whether it would have been better, as
things turned out, to have gone to Perugia in 1945, I am not
sure. I should have gained a deeper insight into the country
and people, perhaps, but seeing them in the immediate aftermath
of war might have implanted misleading first impressions and
prejudices. On balance I am satisfied that my earliest travels in
Italy were with Marian and Jocelyn, and that we all shared the
initial experience of Venice and Rome, Florence and Naples.
Italy after that became the country to which Marian and I
returned again and again, she especially for the art, I for the
history, both of us for the food and wine. Italy came into more
and more of my subsequent books. My first novel after the war,
Snared Nightingale, opened in that most evocative of settings,
the Duke's library at Urbino. My second, *So Wild the Heart*, had
a fictitious lakeside location closely modelled on Sirmione.
Baffled by my inability to find one good history of Italy that
would answer my questions as I pored over the small print in
the Blue Guide, I was driven to do the job myself and write
The Italian Story, covering the whole three thousand years up
to the death of Mussolini. That book, in turn, gave me ideas for
children's books, so that I was not happy until I had used the
Garibaldi campaigns in *Follow My Black Plume* and *A Thousand
for Sicily*. Then, returning to history for adult readers, I wrote
The Grand Tour and *The Condottieri*. The latter sent me back
to my old hero, the good Duke Federigo of Urbino, and I could

not rest till I had visited that palace of his in the little mountain capital, and Mantua with its mournful lagoons where, as a boy hostage, he attended Vittorino da Feltre's famous school. This equipped me to write *Horsemen on the Hills*, an attempt to extend, to the minds of boys and girls, the Urbino spell which had so long held me in its enchantment.

Would this creative sequence have started earlier if the colonel had not so firmly squashed my tentative inquiry? Ironically enough, unknown to either of us, I had given my last talk at Chester.

Ten days later, at half-past four on one of those deceptive Sunday afternoons when it seemed unimaginable that anything could happen at the office, the telephone rang. I was to report at Wakefield next Saturday, as 'waiting man' on an overseas draft. The destination, as was still usual, was secret.

This was a War Office posting, and the colonel at Chester could do nothing about it. For the next few days I was busy clearing up my affairs. I was due for another of my fortnightly visits to the Arts Course. I could have made this final appearance, but time was precious and needed for more urgent things.

'I'll get you off it,' said the sympathetic Dummer. 'They'll understand.' He picked up the telephone and got on the direct line to Western Command. I heard him explaining the situation and emphasising that, while I was perfectly ready to make the journey, it would be appreciated if they would excuse me. He ended, in his kindly, solemn manner, with a remark which I have treasured ever since, and which still sets the echoes of hollow laughter ringing down the years.

'Of course,' said Dummer, looking like an immense khaki-clad owl as he deferentially addressed his unseen superior at Chester, 'of course, sir, *Mr Trease is a soldier first and foremost.*'

CHAPTER NINE

'Passage to More than India'

Two questions were answered within minutes of my walking into the depot at Wakefield: I was no longer 'waiting man' but definitely on the draft, and we were bound for India. And possibly places east, according to the way things developed. It could be, in Walt Whitman's exultant phrase, a 'passage to more than India'.

The thought of India depressed me. Even an English heat-wave laid me flat. I had the left-winger's guilt about the presence of the British there at all. I did not want to face all that famine, disease and squalor. Nor had I much curiosity about ancient Oriental cultures. I was blinkered by my classical education. Europe and the Mediterranean seemed enough for anybody.

There were thirty-six of us on the draft, captains, lieutenants, warrant officers and sergeants. Seldom had so many of the Corps been assembled in one place. To celebrate the occasion a church parade was ordered and we all tramped smartly through the hilly town-centre to the cathedral. The A.E.C. felt a recurrent anxiety to remind the world that its members were combatant soldiers. And now, along with all the vaccination and inoculation and issue of tropical kit, we were handed our arms.

The A.E.C. weapon was the revolver, which happened to be about the only lethal instrument I had never handled during my infantry training. The revolvers had been (I believe) suspended in a bath of oil. They were distributed to us, dripping and un-speakably repulsive. We cleaned them to the accompaniment of muttered imprecations and took note of the number on the specimen assigned to us. They were then, as I remember, taken back and sunk in their oil again. Certainly I was not shown how to load mine, much less to fire it. Now began one of those long anticlimactic waiting periods so inseparable from the military life.

No one knew when our movement order would come; no one knew what to do with us meanwhile. Appropriately for a corps that believed in talks we were given some of our own medicine. A desiccated veteran told us how to comport ourselves in India. When dealing with natives we must at all times respect their *izzit*, or dignity. 'Cheer up,' said the inevitable wag of the party as we left the lecture-room. 'Two years from now your *izzit* will be *wozzit*.' Any joke was better than none.

Incessantly we compared release-group numbers. Some men had such low numbers that it seemed hardly worth while to ship them halfway round the world. I reckoned that with luck even my own Group 31 might be homeward-bound by next Easter.

When we had been given every possible lecture we were left to our own devices. Some played bridge interminably. We read six or seven newspapers, wrote letters, did our laundry. Each morning we clustered round the R.S.M. and heard the unvaried announcement, 'Nothing from the War Office; you can bugger off for the rest of the day.'

Wakefield's attractions were soon exhausted. There was the town theatre with a robust performance of Maugham's *Rain*, the sort of evening that the addicted playgoer, if not the captious critic, can enjoy as honestly as one enjoys cheese and onions. Another night, there was a no less robust Labour meeting in the Town Hall, one of those highly charged, vociferous occasions which television would soon render as sadly rare as the living drama. We were then in the throes of that curious 1945 general election, called by Churchill after Germany's collapse, and the first Britain had known for nearly ten years. It was curious because every citizen, wherever he was serving, was able to vote. Instead of the usual frenzied midnight scenes when the poll was declared, the sealed ballot-boxes would not be opened for weeks, until the remotest elector had had time to express his opinion.

Apart from those two lively evenings, the town offered me nothing more exciting than the inscription on a chemist's shop

where Gissing had been born. Even the most faithful reader of
Henry Ryecroft could not gape at that for ever.

But it was June. There were other places and the days were
long. We went out in small groups and walked the moors. I
visited York, collected my niece from the Mount School, and
climbed the Minster tower with her. One Sunday I rode a
double-decker bus to Leeds, between the endless sooty rhubarb
fields, to visit one of my old Harecroft boys. After tea the
Heppers drove me to a high escarpment, aglow with rhododendrons, looking out over Wharfedale to the misty Forest of
Knaresborough. I stored up such pictures of England. One
never knew which would be the last for some time to come.

At the beginning of July we got our orders. Without a word,
one of the sergeants sat down at the canteen piano and played
'For those in peril on the sea', followed by the Indian Love
Lyrics. We queued up to draw our oily revolvers, wiped them
clean, and stowed them in our holsters. By the next evening we
were aboard the *Capetown Castle*, slipping down Southampton
Water on the most serene of summer evenings. And our
tiresome firearms, needless to say, were in the ship's armoury,
packed in every sense like sardines.

So were we, in at least our economical proximity. The A.E.C.
draft was one tiny group among the several thousand assorted
troops on board. Under peace-time conditions a warrant officer
was entitled to second-class cabin accommodation. We found
ourselves, however, sleeping in what had been the liner's
swimming-pool, deep down below the water-line, in canvas
bunks three or four tiers high, with minimal ventilation and
space to stow our kit. We were better off at meal-times. Then
we still enjoyed our second-class privileges, and ate our way
through menus we had not encountered since 1939.

This half-and-half formula – half peace, half war – was
apparent in other ways. We still had to keep our life-jackets
handy at all times, for, though there was no longer any risk of
German submarines, we might still strike a drifting mine. We
were subject to censorship, and it was not till later that I could
tell Marian either the name of the ship or the route we had
followed. In fact, as the western war was now over, we were
spared the long voyage round the Cape and were able to use the

Suez Canal. It is odd now to look back and remember how in those days we regarded the Canal as Britain's life-line and the Cape route as an intolerable abnormality.

Our Union Castle liner was a fast vessel of recent vintage. In less than three days I was getting my first glimpse of Africa as we approached Gibraltar. The coast looked positively savage in its desolation, the last mountain sloping down to meet the Atlantic with superb finality, the end of a continent. By next day Morocco had (I guessed) turned into Algeria. I scribbled busily.

We pass a town, glistening white, with one immense upstanding tower. The curve of the earth seems to put the houses half submerged beneath the rim of the sea. Only this white tower soars up against shimmering precipices, shadowed with fissures. Curly trails of cloud, like smoke from an engine, hang midway between cliff-crest and sea-level. . . .

People pace the deck, very serious about exercise, clutching books they seldom open. Young officers swot Urdu. The heat affects thought and conversation. . . .

No land in view at all yesterday. This morning, about 6 a.m., crept into Port Said in the morning sunlight. Triangular sails flashed white fins. De Lesseps' statue modestly indicated the Canal ahead. Huge signs proclaimed the presence of British culture, 'Dewar's', 'Johnnie Walker', 'Black and White', while a sweetish smell of putrescent fruit contributed the Oriental atmosphere. We anchored, a flexible pontoon causeway connecting us in zigzags with the palm-fringed land. One or two youths dived in the foul water for 'white money', and, as each coin was retrieved, pouched it in a cheek of apparently infinite capacity. There was a great to-do over hoisting up a melon – the vendor tried to tie it on the end of a two-inch rope, from which it naturally slipped. . . . Egyptian sovereignty was personified in a magnificent policeman at the head of the gangway – white uniform, tasselled red fez, rifle of generous bore, and apparently a cold, to judge by his frequent recourse to his white pocket-handkerchief.

Much beauty in the water and its reflections, here at the

entrance to the Canal. The water normally green, but broken into a thousand ellipses of pure bright blue and, nearer the bank, of restful brown. Sunset behind the strangely perky and upstanding palm-tree tufts. . . . Just after dark we started along the Canal. You couldn't see much. A thin crescent moon was going down in the west. Car-lights raced along the road beside us.

I was surprised by the narrowness of the Canal. The *Capetown Castle* was a big vessel. It seemed a tight fit. During the next day, if some interesting sight drew too dense a crowd to the rails on one side or the other, the loud speakers blared out bidding the human cargo to distribute its weight more evenly.

Tight-packed we certainly were. By this stage of the voyage a strange passion for chess had seized almost everyone on board, and wherever a set could be found or improvised some match was in progress, avidly followed by a craning circle of spectators. Even when we reached the Red Sea, and its July heat transformed our sleeping-quarters into a vibrant oven, men stayed below there playing chess because there was no space on the upper decks.

This phenomenon was due to the magic of one man, probably the most remarkable and certainly the most amusing member of the A.E.C. draft.

Edgar Pennell had become 'Poppa' to us all from the first days at Wakefield. Tall and bald, twinkling and urbane, Poppa had been headmaster of a slum school in Liverpool. He had never played chess until he was thirty, when the boredom of an illness had driven him to the game. Falling instantly under its spell, he had gone back to school and introduced it to his tough young pupils. Soon he had a team playing in county tournaments and holding their own with Liverpool University. The odd thing was that Poppa himself, though an inspired teacher of the game, had none of the aggressive spirit required to win matches, so that he was not himself an outstanding player.

At a Hastings tournament, he told me, he had met the famous John Lewis of the Oxford Street store. Lewis said: 'I want you in my organisation. Staff-training. A man who can teach chess like that can teach anyone anything.' Poppa protested that the idea was ridiculous. He was a headmaster. He knew nothing about business. 'How much do they pay you as a headmaster?' said Lewis. 'I'll give you double. And there'll be opportunities to travel.' Poppa took the job. But the outbreak of war had followed quickly, and, having lost his reserved-occupation status as a headmaster, he was now a warrant officer on the India draft.

In those few days at sea he demonstrated the truth of his story. He had everyone playing chess from the ship's officers to (I can well believe) the ship's cat. His missionary zeal had nothing fanatical about it. He was quiet, modest, humorous and utterly convincing. He would dilate eloquently but sensibly on chess in its philosophic, aesthetic, cultural and character-building aspects. 'It's the one game,' he said, 'where you can't cheat and you can't blame your luck.' He had stories of his old Liverpool pupils – of unprepossessing problem boys who had come over to him with shining eyes, saying, 'Do come an' 'ave a look, sir – look 'ow beautifully 'e beat me!' Poppa loved to play the classic games of the past in his head, Rotlevi *v.* Rubinstein at Lodz in 1907, or even a match that dated back to sixteenth-century Spain. He played them as another man would have played Bach or Beethoven. He was, in fact, intensely musical, proclaimed strongly the triangular affinity of music, chess and mathematics, and explained to me how he could distinguish not only the individual styles of the masters, like composers, but even date the period of a particular game.

If the tedium of those days at sea gave him his most spectacular opportunity for mass-conversion, his finest hour came a little later in India. There he was able to show us the value of chess as a social solvent between the races, even when neither player understood a word of the other's language. With his pocket chess-set Poppa could establish immediate contact with the Indians. He had mastered the differences between the Asian and the European conventions, and he briefed his colleagues on what might otherwise have led to confusion.

There were times when I wondered if I was the only person on board neither playing chess nor waiting my turn for a game. Poppa never tried to convert me. We had many a good talk together, and perhaps that was what he too preferred.

We sailed on. At Suez the sea was a glittering turquoise. Then, as the barbaric coasts receded on either side, the broader waters resumed the blue of the Mediterranean we had left behind. The heat grilled us. We were in shorts now, and even in the shadow of a deck-awning our bare knees burned. One would glance down, thinking that the sun must have crept round unnoticed, and see that one was still in complete shade. But when we reached the Indian Ocean the sky greyed and the ship rolled in the monsoon swell. The A.E.C. draft were by now running talks and discussion-groups. I would stand, fighting nausea, clutching the rail with one hand, trying to interest a platoon of infantrymen who, despite their newly acquired sunburn, looked strangely pale. It was not the ideal moment to hear about the Soviet collective farms or Beveridge's plans for the British welfare state.

So, after two weeks, we caught our first glimpse of Bombay at dawn. It was a cloudy, rain-threatening dawn. The lighthouse was flashing from its tiny rock pedestal. Signals flashed from shore. There was a long white line of surf, like snow. Hills rose and dipped, tufty with palms. There were buoys and lateen sails, smart launches and rust-dappled merchantmen, green sea and ragged brown birds circling the ship. And a solitary butterfly, lemon-coloured.

We packed our kitbags, claimed our revolvers, cleaned off the horrible oil. Then we waited for two whole days, staring at the long waterfront, the domed Taj Mahal hotel, the famous archway known as the Gateway of India. Only one berth, it seemed, would take a vessel as large as ours. It was occupied and we must take our turn.

At long last we were able to edge into the dock, the gangways went down, and after further delays we streamed ashore. The sun was brilliant now after the dullness of recent days; the breeze blew fresh. After seventeen days in the ship, I was prepared to like Bombay.

'Stinking hole', a steward had called it, and no doubt much of it was, but to us it seemed gay and colourful. Blocks of expensive flats, six and seven storey, rose from the Marine Drive, sun-balconied with pastel-tinted walls, green, pink, cream, yellow. Smart De Soto cars stood outside, flashing back the sun.

Prosperous white and off-white residents exercised well-groomed dogs under the coconut palms. Lively children kicked a football in the Oval, dark-skinned sailors from Madras swung by in spot-less white shorts, Mahrati police with flat yellow caps, blue uniforms, and umbrellas ready for the monsoon, signalled the traffic on, lively urchins pestered us to have our shoes cleaned, blackmailing us with a dab of polish threateningly poised on one finger-tip.

Our transit camp at Colaba had long airy huts of brick, complete with charpoys, mosquito-nets, and small red bugs. Hawkers of every kind visited us continually, proffering news-papers, tea, cakes, fruit, prompt laundry-service and other facilities.

My charpoy was a simple wooden bedstead with criss-cross cords to support my bedding, unexpectedly comfortable after the taut canvas of a ship's bunk. Newspapers were a treat we had not enjoyed since Wakefield. All the home news that mattered was in the *Times of India* or the *Statesman*. It was in that hut at Colaba, sipping morning tea in mugs filled by the monotonously chanting char-wallah, that we read the results of the election held three weeks earlier. The Labour landslide was greeted with exultation. If anyone had voted Conservative, he was not saying so. Our papers gave the fullest details. The London *Times* could have told us little more.

Much has been said about the effects of Army Education on the way the troops voted. It would be a mistake to exaggerate the effects of Army Education on anything at all, but there can be no doubt that, where it had a chance to operate, it awakened a fair number of minds to ideas they had never previously entertained. Some instructors may have abused their opportunity to make party propaganda – a Communist would presumably have felt it his higher duty to do so – but I never knew one or heard of any complaints. Most, I fancy, tried to keep their personal sympathies in the background, and stimulate informed discussion as impartially as possible. But the fact was inescap-able: the majority of the Corps must at that date have been more or less Socialist in their individual views. Most of my own colleagues belonged to the National Union of Teachers. The new parliament contained several serving members of the Corps, notably George Wigg. So it may be supposed that the A.E.C. had done little for the preservation of a Tory Britain. Until that morning in Bombay, however, I had never realised the near-unanimity of our own draft.

We stayed only four days in Bombay, just long enough to digest the election news, and then we were off again, aboard the Calcutta Mail, climbing the escarpment of the Western Ghats into the hinterland. We were bound for the Army School of Education (India) which, like its counterpart at Wakefield, combined a training-centre and depot. There we should be acclimatised and otherwise prepared for our new work, before being posted to units in any eastern country where the Army was operating.

We had a hot night journey in third-class carriages, the windows fitted with wire-gauze against mosquitoes and shutters against the sun, the toilet compartment containing only a hole in the floor. Again, the exigencies of war had deprived the British soldier of the comforts he could normally claim. At every station the train was besieged by pathetic multitudes of beggars. We heard, and felt little cause to disbelieve, revolting tales of children deliberately maimed to make them more successful in soliciting alms. They chanted, parrot-fashion, a few words of uncomprehended English. I heard someone wailing over and over again, 'No papa, no mamma, sahib!' and peering down to identify the orphan I saw she was a bent old woman, who looked eighty but (being Indian) need have been no more than fifty.

In the middle of the next day, when the train had not covered half the distance to Calcutta, we got off at Pipariya, where there seemed to be nothing much except a dak bungalow. They served us tea on the verandah while a bus was found for the final stage of our journey. It was a thirty-two-mile drive, at first over a flat, straight, dusty road lined with trees and periodically obstructed with lurching, swerving bullock-carts, their drivers deep in slumber, and latterly up a series of steep and sickening zigzags, through jungle all a-chatter with grey monkeys, and far too often on the unprotected lip of a river gorge.

Pachmarhi, or 'Much-Curry', as our wag promptly renamed it, was the modest summer capital of what was then Central

Provinces, and is now Madhya Pradesh. 'Capital' sounds grand. It was in fact a small hill-station, with a lodge where the provincial governor spent a few of the hottest weeks in the year, and nothing much else but our own military establishment, a government veterinary farm, a civilian club, tennis courts, a golf course, and a local population of a few thousand people, mainly Hindus. But the situation, though it lacked the grandeur I was later to see in the Himalayas, had a wildness of its own.

Our road, the only road there was, climbed through the jungle to a plateau covering nine square miles. Here the altitude averaged 3500 feet. We were level with the top of Snowdon, but the temperature was that of a warm English summer's day. The landscape was open and parklike, dotted with trees. There were some palms and other more exotic specimens, but at times one might have been walking in Sussex. The surprise came when the walk brought one, as it soon did, to the edge of the plateau. There, with a suddenness that caught one's breath, the world fell away into nothing. Sheer precipices went down into the treetops and then that carpet of treetops spread, without break or sign of habitation, to the distant horizon. There were, as I later discovered, paths that wound down to waterfalls and bathing-pools and aboriginal villages. But at first acquaintance our plateau seemed, apart from the one road that had brought us up from Pipariya, as impregnably isolated as Conan Doyle's Lost World. On the third day I was writing:

Have had several short walks. . . . Tremendous precipices and strange upstanding hill-shapes, thickly clothed in jungle – not the palms one imagines, but mainly a semi-English woodland, interspersed with occasional low cacti and clumps of saw-edged grasses. More monkeys and baboons. Vultures over the village slaughterhouse. Low orchids, almost like rhododendron flowers blooming from the ground. . . . A friendly Indian family at the foot of the upper waterfall – the bearded *munshi* (schoolmaster) with wife, sons and daughters, who shared their monkey-nuts with us, with exquisite courtesy. . . . Cave-dwellers, subsisting almost at Neolithic level, a quarter of a mile from the Pearl Talkies Cinema. . . .

The bazaar – A, B, C Streets – nuts, bananas, unidentifiable oddments, photographs, fancy goods, *The Times of India*, Shell-Mex, a shop called 'The Fancy Millinery'. . . . Tailors, watch-repairers by the dozen (apparently), furniture-maker, cobbler, Kashmiri silk merchant, etc. The Urdu Primary School, Beef Market, Mutton Market.

Now, I thought to myself, picking my way through those noisy, stinking lanes, I have seen the Middle Ages. You can clamber about old castles, stare at armour in museums, study illuminated manuscripts – but where in England can you still get the feel of a medieval town?

In India it seemed possible. You had to adjust all the details – not difficult to a practised historical imagination – but the essence was there. Sounds, smells, crowds, insecurity, poverty, disease, superstition . . . these were the common factors.

And so to a great extent, I thought, was the jealous demarcation of trades and duties, though obviously Hindu caste went much deeper than the rivalry of craft and gild. In our quarters we had our bearer, Ram Prashad. But he could not sweep our floor. That was done by a sweeper, an 'untouchable'. Our wood was brought by the *bhisti* and our bath-water by someone else. The *dhobi* called for our laundry, the *dhurzi* came to measure us for suits, the cobbler, the pastry-cook, and the old gentleman who travelled hopefully round with 'sporting goods', comprising one or two fishing-rods and a few coat-hangers, were all at our service and usually looked in upon us about tea-time.

We were quartered in trios in long bungaloid terraces, bare, lofty brick boxes, with sparse but solid furniture, and high bedsteads with mosquito-nets draped over them. The bathroom contained a tin hip-bath, which could be emptied on the concrete floor, there being a hole in the wall that let the water out and might let a cobra in. Snakes were rather attracted to these refreshingly damp holes in walls. After seeing a lengthy specimen dragged out of a neighbour's bathroom and beaten to death, I always took a cautious peep round the door before venturing further, rather as one automatically shook out one's boots before putting them on. Except for the Governor's summer residence, where it was rumoured that a water-closet had somehow been contrived, ours was what future archaeologists will no doubt describe as a chamber-pot culture.

The school could hardly have been in greater contrast to the compact prison-officers' building we had occupied at Wake-field. It was a miscellany of single-storey erections, dotted over a campus of sparse grass and dusty earth. There were the administrative offices, classrooms, a small library, and a grimly barred armoury, sentinelled by ferocious-looking Sikhs, and now containing (needless to say) the revolvers of which we had been carefully relieved on our arrival. I am sorry to go on about those revolvers, but there was a moment when they became relevant. There were, of course, separate officers' and sergeants' messes. The latter was a pleasant place, set in a garden with flaming scarlet flowerbeds, daily watered from a visiting bullock-cart, with long cool verandahs, a good stock of records, and a merry little barman.

This was just the British wing of the school. There were far more Indians, a few hundreds to our few dozens, with their barrack-rooms and dining-halls segregated not only according to rank but also to religion, since Hindu and Muslim could not eat together. The School was a microcosm of the sub-continent. Officers and men had come from units throughout the Indian Army to take short courses so that they could return as educa-tional instructors. Strolling across to the Mess, you might pass several classes grouped under different trees – here a cluster of nippy little Gurkhas, mischievous as English prep-school boys, there a grave conclave of hairy Sikhs, and yonder a circle of pale-skinned, aquiline Punjabis. Not only did their languages vary, but, as a glance at the blackboards showed, so did the alphabets. But at this date, thanks to Winston Churchill's personal enthusiasm for Basic English, that was the study most in vogue. Whatever the class, its members were most likely to be bellowing at each other like gutteral parrots, 'This – is – my *finger!* This – is – my *nose!*' and making gestures that were, to a western eye, at least ambiguous.

Presiding over the whole establishment was our Comman-dant, Colonel Newey, an impressive if slightly histrionic character with the rare pale-blue cap-band of his rank and twenty-three years' experience of India. His welcoming address to us showed that he was a man who loved public speaking and had studied the technique. Some laughed at him and called him pompous. So he was, at times, but he was always easy to listen to and a good heart beat under that carefully out-thrust chest. He loved India and was anxious that we should see and learn as much as we could while we were in the country. He appreciated that we were essentially civilians, reluctant visitors, anxious to get home, which was more than some of his staff, long-service regulars, could ever comprehend. He never held it against us. They hated our guts.

'And always remember,' Newey counselled us, lifting an admonitory finger, 'never strike an Indian, whatever the provocation. Oh, you might have to defend yourself if he came at you in some brawl, but even then, be careful, don't give him a punch *here*.' He tapped his well-filled tunic. 'A blow there wouldn't do any harm to an Englishman. But these people have all had malaria; it may have left them with an enlarged spleen. You could kill a man without meaning to.'

Newey's orations always contained something unforgettable.

Even the more pedestrian lectures given by the other officers were preferable to the Urdu lessons we now reluctantly began. There was a good chance that we should be posted to some unit where Urdu would not be needed. I had exhausted most of my own capacity for languages while at school, and now, with my thirty-sixth birthday looming, I felt little enthusiasm for an Oriental tongue I should never master. It was not even a respectable Oriental language. Army Urdu was a bastard tongue, liberally sprinkled with unaltered English words, so that 'Clean your rifle' became '*Rifle saf karo*'. I could never take Urdu seriously after one morning when I had to attend a British major on his routine inspection. The cantonment was well provided with urinals and latrines, the former consisting often of a row of homely utensils on a plank, for the geology of the plateau, and the importance of keeping the wells uncontaminated, made such provision essential. The major was dissatisfied with what he found. Emerging, he bellowed at a terrified old sweeper fifty yards away, and then, tapping the enamel vessel emphatically, and rather musically, with his cane, he delivered the remark that effectively finished my interest in Oriental languages: '*Piss-pot saf karo!*'

Even before that, events in the wider world had drastically modified our attitude to our studies. We had reached Pachmarhi on 28 July. In our second week the newspapers brought word of the first atomic bomb dropped on Hiroshima, of Russia's declaration of war on Japan two days later, and of the second bomb dropped on Nagasaki. We knew none of the horrific details. The more scientific among us, or the better informed, may have guessed and may have pondered the implications for the future of the world, but most, like myself, had no thought beyond relief and joy at the shortening of the war. A few days later, on 15 August, we were celebrating VJ-Day. All drinks in the Mess were free and the Corps showed that, in one respect at least, it could hold its own with the less-intellectual branches of the service.

When the fumes of cheap Indian gin had somewhat evaporated and the floors had ceased to tilt under our feet, it was possible, if not to see our future more clearly, at least to make better-informed guesses. We should see no fighting. We should be dealing with large bodies of troops who now had time on their hands, while, like ourselves, they awaited their turn for demobilisation and a ship to take them home. Some of us might be working with released prisoners from the Japanese camps.

As the weeks of our own course drew to an end, the Chief Instructor bade us fill up forms which, remarkably for army documents, gave us a chance to express personal preferences for where we would like to go. It was hard not to feel that the millennium was near. In the past few months we had witnessed the defeat of Germany, the Conservatives and Japan. Now the Army was consulting us on our own future. The mind reeled.

'There are so few of you,' said the Chief Instructor, 'and you'll be in such demand everywhere, you should be able to get the postings you want. But just give your second preference to be on the safe side.'

India, I had decided, was altogether too big and complex for a stay as short as mine seemed likely to be. It would stand me in much better stead as a writer if I acquired experience of some smaller, more unified country. I had always felt a vague attraction to Ceylon. I wrote 'Ceylon'. Since my arrival in Pachmarhi I had read several interesting booklets about the constructive work done in Punjabi rural areas, the 'village uplift' movement started by some benign British officer to sink wells, combat erosion, improve the soil, teach hygiene, and generally anticipate the good work done by international agencies a generation later. This appealed to me as a subject I could learn something about in less than a lifetime. So I put 'Punjab' as second choice.

The Chief Instructor glanced down my form approvingly. 'You should be pretty certain of one or the other,' he said.

Some weeks later the postings came from Command and I read the typewritten list on the board. W.O.Instr. Class II R. G. Trease was retained on the permanent staff.

CHAPTER TEN

Author's Notes

M y disappointment did not last long. Eventually, as news of my late companions trickled back, I realised how lucky I had been.

The sudden victory had created more military muddle than usual. Some A.E.C. men never found the formations to which they had been posted. Units had merged, moved, or – one was tempted to believe – never existed. Only a handful of our draft did much useful work in the East. More time was spent in hopeful travelling from place to place without ever arriving anywhere in time to catch the people who had once, presumably, requested their services. The most resentful, however, were those posted to the George V schools, where Indian boys were being educated on English public-school lines. These A.E.C. men were qualified teachers whose posts were being kept open for them at home, where they were badly needed. They had not minded being conscripted into an army at war, but they objected passionately to remaining as conscripted schoolmasters teaching Indian children. I saw their point, especially when Marian wrote that Jocelyn was in a class of forty-seven at Abingdon.

At Pachmarhi I had an interesting, mildly useful, not too onerous job to do. I became a sort of sergeant-major to the British Wing, though without any of the bellowing parade-ground connotations of that post. I had to welcome and docu-ment the parties arriving at frequent intervals, A.E.C. drafts from Britain and men from various units already in India who were taking short courses for educational duties. Interesting individuals were apt to turn up. Once, gathering up the forms they had just completed, I was struck by the incongruous juxta-position of 'Courses attended: Street-fighting' and 'Special qualifications: Chopin Medallist'. The name was Lieutenant

John Vallier, the concert pianist. We struck up a pleasant, if all
too brief, acquaintanceship. He came over to tea in my bungalow
– I had much better quarters now I was on the staff – and we
compared the problems of a young writer and a young musician
struggling for recognition.

Paperwork came in fits and starts. Between arrivals, there
was little. Even the Major to whom I was directly responsible,
and who eyed me with extreme suspicion and distaste, could
find me no further occupation in the office, and, beyond making
me escort him on his tour of kitchens and latrines, left me
largely to my own devices. The Commandant, on the other
hand, found me plenty to do. I was to prepare lectures on the
history of the British in India, I was to lecture on Russia, I was
to lead walking parties, and I was to organise the weekly
play-reading.

Newey adored play-reading. He was a frustrated actor and
made up for it in every waking moment, but only in a play-
reading could he really let himself go. Before the war, he told
me, he had taken part in radio-plays broadcast from Bombay,
assisted by his wife and daughter. Mrs Newey was still available, and I was left in no doubt as to the importance of casting her appropriately. Usually her husband saved me the
trouble.

'Ah, Mr Trease,' he would say, handing me a sheaf of typed
scripts, 'here is the play for Monday. *I* shall be Shakespeare,
Mrs Newey will be Queen Elizabeth, *you* will be Bacon.' Then,
after a perfectly timed pause and with a regal gesture. 'You
may cast the other characters yourself.'

After he had heard me lecture on Russia I had to prepare a
special talk on Soviet Asia for the information of Indian officers,
and then write an article for the wall-newspaper in the Indian
Wing. 'But clear it first with Ginger Whiskers,' he warned me.
'It's so easy to offend Muslim susceptibilities.'

Ginger Whiskers was, more formally, Risaldar-Major
Sheikh Surajjudin Bahadur, a veteran Punjabi cavalryman who
was finishing his army service as R.S.M. to the Indian Wing.
He owed his nickname to his brilliant henna-dyed beard, sign
that he had made the Mecca pilgrimage. He was Newey's
spiritual adviser on Islam. He was a delightful man, his natural

dignity and humility perfectly blended, and Newey's trust was
repaid with a respect that bordered on reverence. 'Thanks to
God and Colonel Newey,' he remarked unforgettably, when
publicly acknowledging the conferment of his O.B.I.

His public utterances were apt to be unforgettable, for
though he spoke fluent English he often sounded an 'o' as an
'a', while omitting to sound an 'h' at all. This could be unfortunate when he dropped into reminiscences of his early days in
Skinner's Horse. There was an evening, too, when John Vallier,
having himself expertly tuned the piano, treated us to a Chopin
recital. I noticed Ginger Whiskers' enjoyment – I saw the
light kindled in those fierce Punjabi eyes and the rhythmic
jigging of his foot during the livelier passages. When Vallier
had given us the last possible encore, Ginger Whiskers was
called upon to express our thanks for the entertainment. 'The
music carried me back to my young days in the cavalry,' he
said emotionally. 'I fancied myself once more sitting on my
horse – ' It was a great relief that we were able to break into
renewed clapping at this point.

Ginger Whiskers thoroughly approved my article on Soviet
Asia. He was not even worried, as Newey had feared, by my
reference to the Soviet abolition of polygamy. Many Indian
Muslims, he assured me, were monogamous. It was all most
men could do to support one wife. What I had written would
upset nobody. He then treated me to an exposition of the Koran's
teaching on marriage, referring gravely to Wife A, Wife B,
Wife C and Wife D, and their minimum entitlement to their
husband's favours of once a month each. But all that, he inferred,
concerned only an opulent minority.

Chats with Ginger Whiskers were only one medium whereby
I gained a little insight into Indian life. Newey, zealous that
every newcomer from Britain should use his time profitably,
arranged introductions and visits to the local school and the
government office controlling the affairs of our isolated community. After meeting the Naib Tehsildar, an agreeable
Pooh-Bah character who combined the functions of magistrate,
town clerk, food controller and chief constable, I was shocked to
learn how poorly he was paid. He was an M.A. and a barrister-
at-law. For his numerous duties he received the monthly

salary of 200 rupees, or exactly what I, as a British sergeant-major, drew in addition to my free food and quarters. In this case he was probably an honest man – he admitted he had to borrow money from relatives to educate his family. But the difficulties, temptations, and opportunities of his job could be imagined. He was, however, a plutocrat compared with his police-constables. *Their* pay varied, according to length of service, from 15 to 22 rupees per month. The newsagent in the bazaar had to supply the police with a list of all his subscribers and what papers they bought.

Teachers seemed to be as ill-paid as policemen – and many turned to more lucrative occupations. The man who came round our bungalows every afternoon, peddling cakes, was a former *munshi*. The Pachmarhi school itself, however, seemed to be a happy place with an enthusiastic staff. It ranked as relatively 'progressive'. There were twelve girls as well as the eighty boys, and they were allowed to sit in full view of each other. Muslims, Hindus and a few Christians sat together in the crowded desks. On the walls, along with crude pictures of the royal family and war posters, were mottoes such as BE POLITE and LEARN TO OBEY, but the children were encouraged to hold debates.

And concerts. I shall not forget the concert I attended. The back of the hall was curtained off by a long white sheet. Behind this sat the mothers. When the show started they lifted it shyly and peered beneath.

But in the show the young girls played their full part, dancing and singing in their thin nasal voices against a background of incredibly garish and hideous magnificence. There was a butterfly dance, the butterflies stamping barefoot with a resonance that went ill with their gossamer wings.

The boys – some of them – were much more beautiful than the girls. They had a greater delicacy of feature, less flatness, and the same liquid eyes. Handsome or ugly, they were born comedians. Both sexes were brilliantly expressive in gestures. I especially remember the monologue of the boy who flung away his mosquito-net and repellent cream, complaining that because of them he no longer missed school through illness. And the anti-Japanese drama with the patriotic refrain,

'*Hindustan hamara hai!*' ('India is ours'). They were young children. The concert lasted from 8.30 till 11 p.m.

The schoolmistress-prompter hovered frantically in the wings throughout – schoolmistresses and prompters seemed to be much the same, the world over. But the blowing of a whistle, to mark changes in the choreography, was at least novel. The music was monotonous and no doubt it was difficult to synchronise the changes in any other way.

Four days later I was watching a more traditional entertainment, the Hindu festival of Desara. The drums were already beating when I walked down to the bazaar just before sunset. The goddess Durga rode aloft on a tall structure reminiscent of a Punch and Judy show. This stood on a trailer, manhandled a few yards forward every time a whistle blew. They were great on whistles at Pachmarhi. Ahead of the goddess more men kept a square space clear with a rope, and in this shifting arena the tiger dance was re-enacted every time the procession stopped.

The 'tigers' were men, or often quite small boys, with caps of tiger or leopard skin, fearsomely clawed gauntlets, and long curly tails so springy that they must have been based on wire. The dancers wore only loin-cloths. Their bodies were elaborately painted, not only with tiger stripes but with pictures of wild beasts. They postured and crouched in pairs, rhythmically.

In another part of the bazaar small boys were twirling staves around their heads with lightning speed and unbelievable dexterity. This proved to be only a juvenile foretaste of what was to come. As darkness fell, the performance was taken up by men, but now the whirling staves had great masses of flaming tow attached to both ends. With an almighty hiss and roar these fiery dumb-bells swung through the air, lighting up the glistening bodies of the dancers, the rapt faces ringing them. Now and again a blazing fragment flew off into the crowd. Once, a little girl's sari was caught. Hastily, but without undue concern, the bystanders extinguished her. The dance went on.

Diwali, two or three weeks later, was quite different, a Hindu family festival, with shops closed and everyone indoors. The houses were illuminated with scores of little lamps ranged in lines along verandahs, on window-sills and in alcoves. The lamps were no more than brown earthenware saucers, with a fat wick, like a slug, trailing over the rim, but the total effect, lighting up the façades with a warm orange glow, held a delicate enchantment.

All this was in the urban and relatively sophisticated atmosphere of Pachmarhi. A few miles away, down in the jungle beneath the plateau-rim, it was still possible to see aborigines living very much the same existence as a hundred – or a thousand – years earlier. The plateau itself had been theirs until it was discovered by a Captain J. Forsyth as recently as 1862. The establishment of a British hill-station, with its inevitable influx of shopkeepers and others, had pushed the unfortunate Korkus into the forest below, where they survived under the protection of the Government. They could not even be visited without a permit from the Naib Tehsildar, but this was issued at a nod from Newey, who was keen that we should see this aspect of Indian life as well. The two excursions I regularly led were the ascent of Dhupgarh, an easy mountain walk since the summit, at 4429 feet, was only a thousand feet higher than the School itself, and the descent to the aborigines' settlement at Rori Ghat. I took particularly full notes, feeling that they would be useful some day, as they were in *The Young Traveller in India.*

Today we walked to Rori Ghat, a dozen of us – a rough five miles from where we left the truck on the lip of the plateau, close under Dhupgarh. Glorious scenery in the mouth of the pass through which we went down – blue shadows and green rugged shagginess, shady twists and turns over a sandy bouldery trail, tall mango-trees, clustered bamboos, a grey stream splashing down over grey stones between grey trunks – almost Welsh. . . . Later, as we came out on the hillside and saw the green patches of field below us, more than one of us thought of Cumberland – the brighter green of the dale-head as one comes down from the fells. . . .

There are about 150 Korkus, 25 families in as many huts. They speak a debased Hindi and have a debased Hindu religion, complete with caste system. They bury their dead, except the rich ones, because only the rich can afford the wood for burning. (This in the middle of the jungle! But it is State Forest, and the right to cut wood must be paid for.) They carve memorial slabs, depicting a man's property. The sun or moon shows whether he died in the daytime or at night. These slabs are carried to the sacred mango-tree at Pachmarhi and deposited.

They have crops, and sell a surplus in the bazaar, where they have to buy their kerosene oil, etc. They gather wild mangoes and pound the kernels into flour. They have about 100 cattle and buffaloes between them, also hens. Yet they are very poor, and the children, not having enough clothes to keep warm at night, cluster round an all-night fire. When the crops fail, they go out and work on the roads or at other jobs on the plateau. The headman gets about ten rupees, or fifteen shillings, per year from the Government for his services. He is the only literate.

A doctor is supposed to visit monthly – he has been only once in five months, and then because detailed by a higher authority, after a cholera scare. . . .

They came to meet us down a trodden lane of flowering hedges. They brought charpoys and great lengths of stout bamboo matting, on which we sat to eat our lunch under the banyan tree, watched by the assembled males. The houses varied but on the whole were pretty miserable – thatched roofs and bamboo screens for walls. Naked, pot-bellied children stared from the doorways – there was no cry for baksheesh – and women, heedless of our visit, continued their interminable pounding and grinding at the rear.

It was impossible, our guide explained to us, to convince the Korkus that these visiting groups of white sahibs were not important government officials. They came up and poured out sad complaints and petitions. The villagers were troubled by a man-eating tiger and would like us to do something about it.

'Well, we can report it,' I said to our guide. 'Whereabouts does it usually operate?'

'Oh, anywhere in that part of the jungle, sahib.' He waved his hand airily towards the dense forest through which we had just walked, and through which we now had to return, without any kind of a gun between us. We did not saunter on the way back, and were not sorry to regain the more open country of the plateau. Tigers did not trouble us there, but leopards prowled quite near the cantonment.

My writing was not confined to the jottings in my notebook. There was a fair amount of intermittent leisure that autumn, and, with one side of a bungalow entirely to myself – bathroom, bedroom, living-room and verandah facing straight across the treetops far below – I enjoyed a privacy I had not known since joining the Army. Best of all, I was able to spirit away a surplus typewriter from the office and a supply of foolscap.

Muriel Burton, now with the B.B.C. in Manchester, told me that the head of Northern Children's Hour, Nan Macdonald, wanted short stories with Indian settings. I have always found short stories difficult. They are not really, as runners say, my distance. Like poems, they demand inspiration. While I have often promised a full-length book before I had an idea for its plot, I have never dared to accept a short-story commission until the outline was clear in my head. Luckily, in this case, the exotic setting of the plateau and the odd characters peopling it gave me the ideas. My first effort, 'Flit-Wallah', was inspired by a dusky imp of about ten, who bore that title in real life, and also bore, most proudly, a flit-gun with which he perambulated the cantonment, spraying the places most attractive to flies. Flit-Wallah's real story and character remained unknown – we had no means of communication but a friendly grin and wave – but to weave fiction around that jaunty little figure was easy enough. This story marked my début as a radio-writer, and in after years it was often reproduced in anthologies. It was the first of several that I wrote during those months, all set in Pachmarhi, and Nan Macdonald took them all.

Mostly my writing was devoted to another junior historical novel for Blackwell. At Leamington I had read the early volumes of Churchill's *Marlborough* and decided that some day I must re-tell for children the exciting events of the Glorious Revolution. Whig politics aside, another aspect of the period attracted me. My work in Army Education had done something to deepen my interest, uninformed though it was, in music. The English, I felt, were too ready to underrate the contribution their nation had made in this field, too willing to agree that, unlike the Welsh and Italians, they were by nature deficient. I had an urge to tell modern children that there had been one period at least when England – the England of Pepys and Purcell – had been second to no country in Europe in its love of music-making. When I observed a particularly convenient coincidence of dates, that the first performance of the first English opera, *Dido and Aeneas*, had fallen within a few months of William of Orange's triumphal entry into London, it was obvious that the two themes would interweave. That the performance had taken place at a girls' boarding-school in Chelsea seemed an almost unbelievable bonus for a writer of children's fiction. What provided me with my central idea, however, was Jeremiah Clarke's 'Trumpet Voluntary', which had leapt into popularity during the war. There was a romantic pathos in the thought that poor Clarke was remembered, more than two centuries after his suicide, for just one composition that lasted only a few minutes, yet stirred millions who now heard it. My hero, I decided, should be an imaginary musician of that period, winning immortality through a similarly brief 'Martial Air for Trumpets'. There the resemblance would stop. My Jack Norwood would find fulfilment as a performer, on the violin, and another kind of happiness with the Chelsea schoolgirl who had sung Belinda in the opera. No call for suicide.

Through that autumn I wrote steadily, posting the type-script to Marian four foolscap sheets at a time, the maximum weight that we could send post-free by Forces Air Mail. Not one instalment went astray. When the tally was complete, she took the book into Oxford and delivered it to Henry Schollick at Blackwell. He was not a publisher given to effusive encourage-ment of his authors, but he told her it was the best thing I had yet done.

Research was my chief problem. If my years in the Education Corps had taught me nothing else, they had impressed upon me the moral obligation to know one's facts and to present them fairly. If I had been posted to any other unit in India I should scarcely have dared to tackle a story demanding much back-ground reading. Even the School of Education had only a modest library of books and I was not exaggerating when I confessed in an author's note:

I have had just three books to refer to, and I am very grateful to them all – Macaulay's *History of England*, W. J. Turner's *English Music*, and Eric Blom's *Music in England*. I have had just one record of Purcell's music to inspire me, while for distraction I have had monkeys chattering outside my window by day and buffaloes moaning like fog-horns by night. So it was seldom easy (but always pleasant) to imagine myself in the England of 1688.

Pleasant? Perhaps a little more than pleasant. Sometimes, during those solitary months, the steady writing of *Trumpets in the West* served as a psychological lifeline. More than twenty-five years later I was lecturing at a college of education in Wales and was rather taken aback by one student's contribution to the discussion. 'All through the story,' she said, 'I was struck – and rather puzzled – by the pervading undercurrent of melancholy. I only understood when I got to your Author's Note at the end.'

I had never realised that it had come through, even in an adventure story. Of course – inevitably – there had been times on those solitary evenings at Pachmarhi when one stood on one's verandah overlooking the jungle-choked ravine and stared at the great silly moon swimming up over those fantastic hill-formations and could almost have howled at it like a dog.

CHAPTER ELEVEN

'British, Go Home!'

In my notebook, amid all the jotted observations of Indian life and scenery – 'scarlet flowers of the gnarled and leafless red silk cotton-tree', 'crested woodpecker with red dragoon-like plume', and 'woman with vivid mustard sari, scarlet-edged', there is a cryptic entry dated 27 September 1945:

> Sent for by C. In event of certain (unlikely) contingency, to find him at once wherever he is, to remain at his side whatever happens, and to keep hour-by-hour diary, each page signed. 'If as President of the Cantonment Board I appeal to myself as O.C. Station. . . . ' (An appeal unlikely to fall on deaf ears.)

This was all I thought it discreet to record in writing of a somewhat melodramatic conversation with Newey ('C' standing for 'Commandant') soon after my appointment to the staff.

Having peered round to ensure that neither the Indian Chief Clerk, Mr Gaddi, was in earshot, nor any of his minions, Newey dropped his voice and explained his urgent summons.

'Until lately, Trease, I would have said with confidence that, wherever else in the country trouble started, Pachmarhi would be the last place – the *last* place. Now' – and he fixed me with a stern eye – '*I no longer feel that confidence.*'

It was not, he hastened to assure me, that the local people wanted the British to go. Trouble, if it came, would come from our ever-changing population of Indian troops, drawn from every corps and regiment and incarnating every religious and racial animosity that made the Indian problem so intractable. In the past, military discipline, impartial British officers, and the natural comradeship of active service, had kept these differences submerged. Now the Indianisation of even the higher commissioned ranks, the end of the war, and the general feeling that the British were on their way out were combining to bring them bubbling to the surface. The risk was that the Indian troops would start fighting among themselves and the British would have to intervene. Since at Pachmarhi the only British troops were a handful of A.E.C. instructors, plus a few dozen other short-term visitants on a course or a draft – the total outnumbered at least ten to one by Indian troops – the prospect was cheerless.

What had shaken Newey was a trivial incident, when a Muslim had walked into a Hindu mess-hut (or the other way round – I forget which) and had picked up a piece of meat. This, said Newey, could have provoked a lynching or a mass riot or both. Only Newey's prompt and diplomatic action had saved the situation. The offender had been smuggled out of Pachmarhi and returned to his unit. But one never knew when something similar might occur again.

'It needs only a spark,' he said dramatically. 'The whole place could go up in a matter of minutes. So. . . . '

'Yes, sir?'

'You will provide yourself with a notebook. In that you will keep the Diary of the Incident.'

At the first news of trouble – 'a shot in the bazaar, for instance' – I was to seize notebook and pencil, clap on my steel helmet, mount the office bicycle, and pedal heroically in quest of Newey. Nothing was said about getting my revolver. Presumably it was still in the barred and padlocked armoury, guarded by those ferocious-looking Sikhs. On the whole, I privately reflected, it might be safer to go unarmed than to ask for it back. Whose side would the Sikhs be on?

'Then, Trease, under my direction, you will write down the exact sequence of events. It might go something like this: "09.00 hrs, shots heard from the bazaar. 09.20 hrs, the President of the Cantonment Board requests O.C. Station for the use of troops." As I am both – ' Newey permitted himself to smile. His passion for the theatre included an appreciation of comic relief. He went on, grave again: 'It is most important to get the

times precise – for any subsequent inquiry. Especially matters
like the order to open fire, when fire was actually opened, when
it ceased, and so on.'

And who, I wondered to myself, would make the entry – and
in what notebook – 'Colonel Newey and W.O. Trease tipped
over edge of the plateau at 11.30 hrs'?

'And remember,' he broke in on these personal reflections,
working up to a climax so that the curtain could descend
effectively upon the scene, 'you are to mention this conversation
to nobody. *Nobody!* You understand?'

'Yes, sir.' And metaphorically pulling my hat over my eyes
and muffling myself in my cloak I slunk away.

It was not, I think, after this conversation but when I had been
seen coming down from the Commandant's verandah after a
more mundane discussion – probably about a walking party or
a play-reading – that I entered my own office across the road to
meet the Major positively distended with repressed fury.

'Mr Trease! You have just come from the Commandant's
office?'

'Yes, sir.'

'Did he send for you?'

'No, sir, but I had to see him about – '

'In future, Mr Trease, you will have the goodness to ask
my permission before going to see the Commandant. You
understand?'

'Very good, sir.'

I should never understand, and would never wish to understand, how the petty niceties of military protocol could be
taken seriously by the members of a corps like ours, all supposed
to be men of some intelligence and culture. But I did understand
that the Major hated my guts.

It was not only among the Indian troops that the end of the
war had released previously suppressed jealousies. It was
happening among ourselves, between regulars like the Major
and temporary soldiers like myself. Many of these regulars,
now holding war-time commissions, had been themselves
sergeants and warrant officers before 1939 – they had begun as
'army schoolmasters' of the old type, with modest qualifications
and few opportunities in stations like Malta and Gibraltar to

develop cultural interests. During the past few years they had found themselves working uneasily with subordinates of very different backgrounds and experience, Oxford or Cambridge graduates, schoolmasters, college lecturers, with the occasional lawyer, journalist or author. This co-operation they had accepted with as good a grace as possible, many indeed, like Dummer, with relief and gratitude, since it helped them to keep afloat when they were out of their depth. Now, however, just as we conscripts longed for our return to what we regarded as 'real' life, they could scarcely wait for a return to 'real' education. I remember one of these regular captains – a nice man, but of limited horizons – informing me gleefully of some new directive from on high. 'Thank God,' he said, 'we're getting back to *real* education.' I asked him how he defined it. 'The three Rs,' he said, 'Empire history, and map-reading.' Current affairs, cultural activities and citizenship, which he saw as Socialist propaganda, were on their way out.

The Major could not hide his glee when he told me that I was to parade before breakfast for a refresher course in small-arms training. The handful of A.E.C. men were to be formed into a platoon, so that, in an emergency, if we could not restore order, we could at least sell our lives dearly, or with luck defend ourselves until help came from Jubbulpore, a long way distant on the plain.

In this forlorn hope I was to have the honour of commanding a section. Privately, I did not see how this could combine with my special role as Newey's squire and scribe, keeping the Diary of the Incident. Nor did I see how I could explain to the Major that I was not available, since Newey had sworn me to secrecy about my assignment. On the other hand, how could I explain to Newey, and get my lips unsealed, when the Major had expressly forbidden me to speak to the Commandant except through him?

To solve this problem neatly called for the ingenuity of a Gilbert. I did not possess it. I did, however, have a great reluctance to get up an hour earlier in the mornings. So, after obediently turning out for the first of the parades, I took a chance and, without asking the Major's permission, sought an audience with the Most High.

'I am embarrassed, sir,' I said, all poker-faced and a soldier first and foremost, while inwardly gloating, 'for I can't tell Major X what *you* have told me to do, and *he* has previously instructed me. . . .'

It was a golden opportunity to convey to the Commandant what it had been impossible to indicate before, that the Major wished to obstruct any direct communication between us.

'Don't worry,' said Newey. 'You have acted quite properly. There is no point in parading with the others if you aren't going to be available. I will speak to Major X.'

I was ordered on no more pre-breakfast weapon-training.

How petty it all seems in retrospect! Yet as a writer I found such experiences profitable. The full-time author is envied for his freedom, but he pays a price for his insulation from the working relationships of other men. For most of my life I have not known what it is to take orders or to give them. Only the Army compelled me to endure bureaucracy from the inside, to feel the humiliations and frustrations generated by differences of rank, and to enjoy the compensating pleasure of mild intrigue and manœuvre. These are the common stuff of every historical period, and the historical story-teller needs the basic experience, which he can then transmute into forms quite unrecognisable. So, after a skirmish with the Major, I might walk off to my bungalow, sit down and slip a sheet of office foolscap into my W.D. typewriter – lucky he did not know about *that*! – and dash off at white heat the chapter in *Trumpets in the West* where my musician, Purcell's protégé, clashes with the titled ignoramus who offers him condescending patronage. Even if Major X had looked over my shoulder, he would not have seen himself in the 'paunchy, purple-cheeked' Lord Bablocke with his 'fine buckled shoes and white-stockinged calves like pillars', but he had unwittingly made his contribution to the book all the same.

Curiously enough, though my very first books, *Bows Against the Barons* and *Comrades for the Charter*, had won me the reputation of writing for the under-dog, I had never felt in the slightest degree an under-dog myself until – occasionally – then. Lack of money might be an inconvenience, but it had never been a source of shame. I knew there was a vast social superstructure of people with wealth, influential connections and famous pedigrees, but if, for convenience, I thought of them as an 'upper' class, it never occurred to me that I was, by corollary, 'inferior' to them or to any man alive. Even my months as an infantry private had failed to sow any doubts in my mind, but certainly army life, and above all army life in India, deepened my empathy with the under-dogs of every land and period. I never saw this empathy as in any way inconsistent with a scrupulous regard for the historical facts.

In that autumn of 1945 the British Raj – had we but known it – had less than two years to run. Some people were still behaving as though it had two hundred. Japan had been beaten, Mr Attlee and his Labour Government were far away, let it be 'back to normal'. At times the British civilians were far more reactionary than the military. There was a caste system as rigid, if not as publicly recognised, as the Hindu. The British businessman deferred, with whatever ill grace, to the commissioned officer and made up for it by his contempt for the 'British Other Rank'. In Darjeeling I saw the announcement of a dance:

GENTLEMEN	Rs.2.
B.O.R.s	1.8.
LADIES	Free.

It was something that the B.O.R.s were allowed to mix with the 'ladies' and 'gentlemen'. At the Pachmarhi Club it would still have been unthinkable. There it was the civilian members, we were assured, who kept the door shut against us.

This was no serious deprivation, but at New Year it proved somewhat embarrassing.

We were so small a British community on the plateau that any clash of festive arrangements was best avoided. So, as Christmas approached, and goodwill was in the air, an amicable committee meeting was held to co-ordinate the programme. I attended as President of the Sergeants' Mess. As our Saturday dances were a regular institution, attended by officers and their wives, and open to all, it was at once agreed that New Year's Eve should be our responsibility and that no other function should be arranged for that night.

For this occasion, and the preceding festivities of the season, the Mess was imaginatively decorated. One of our sergeants, Charles Barker, was an artist in ordinary life, and Newey with his usual flair had grabbed him for the permanent staff to take charge of Arts and Crafts. Poor Charles had had a frustrating autumn, for the teaching of these subjects to Indians was full of complications unknown in England. Leatherwork, so popular in British units, was unthinkable to a Hindu. Muslims, Newey warned him, might be shocked by any representation, however artistic, of human nudity. And Indians in general tended to despise basketry, woodwork, or any type of handicraft, as fit only for low-class persons and unsuitable for an educated man. So it was with some relief that Charles flung himself into the uninhibiting assignment of Christmas décor for the Mess.

The traditional, sentimental motifs were ignored. Instead of snow we had sea-gulls, hundreds of paper sea-gulls dangling from the ceiling. The bar was transformed into a pirate ship, and the marine atmosphere was carried out in everything.

Christmas itself was a great success, though it was the sort of gastronomical marathon – or pentathlon – I would not undertake again. Our bearers, waking us with the usual morning tea, festooned us with garlands of pungent double marigolds. Within an hour or two of breakfast we were on our way to the equivalent Indian mess, that of the Viceroy-commissioned officers. As both Hinduism and Islam forbade alcohol, their hospitality necessarily took the form of mid-morning coffee or tea, accompanied by mounds of sticky Oriental sweetmeats, which we had to consume liberally in the interests of inter-racial camaraderie. At noon we hurried back to our own mess, where we were entertaining the Commandant and British officers to pre-lunch drinks.

When Newey and his wife departed, and protocol permitted the others to follow, we sat down to our Christmas dinner. The rations included a small tinned pudding for every two men. The cook conscientiously sent in each plate with a semicircular wodge that would have satisfied a young family. Somehow we managed to stand at the appropriate moment and drink the health of the King-Emperor.

Afternoon memories are hazy. We sauntered to the cinema, where the little gallery, furnished with cane chaises-longues, was reserved for Europeans at the twice-weekly shows of British films. We saw Coward's *This Happy Breed*. Ginger Whiskers told me afterwards how much he and his compatriots had enjoyed it. The mother-in-law problem, he explained, was international. Of course, he had not liked it quite so much as Olivier's *Henry V*, which had revived so many happy memories of Skinner's Horse. . . .

We strolled back to our quarters, wondering how we could face a second Christmas dinner in the Officers' Mess, where we were bidden for eight. A cup of tea would clear our heads, and this need had been anticipated by our bearers. . . . Grinning lovably, they fussed in with the 'special tea' they had laboured to prepare in honour of the sahibs' religious festival. There were sardines and other delicacies.

On the following day, it was pleasant to think of other people's stomachs. The Sergeants' Mess put on a tea-party for the little girls of a Eurasian boarding-school. Charles Barker's sea-gulls were a great success. So was Santa Claus, who drove up to the building in traditional red coat and cotton-wool whiskers but with a bullock-cart instead of a reindeer-sleigh. Unfortunately, at the most impressive moment of his arrival, a yapping mongrel rushed out and frightened the bullock, which lashed out and gave Santa a kick on the thigh as he stepped down. Santa was in considerable anguish for some time afterwards, but heroically completed his distribution of presents with all the cheerful banter expected of him.

The festive programme was going splendidly. I looked forward confidently to the New Year's Eve dance which would be the last of my responsibilities.

That morning I learned that, despite our previous agreement, there was to be a party at the Pachmarhi Club. As we conscripts had no wives on the station, our weekly dances depended entirely on the attendance of officers and their ladies, civilians, and anyone staying at the leave-centre. The very shortage of partners contributed to the zest of the occasion.

There would not be much zest if there were no partners at all. I went hot-foot to the Major, stamped my hot feet, and accorded him a salute whose very quiver reflected the vibrations within me. Yes, he admitted with some awkwardness, it was true.

There was to be a New Year's Eve party at the Club after all.

'Then, sir, we had better cancel our dance. It will be impossible.'

'Oh, no, Trease. Go ahead. It will be quite all right. The officers will mostly be coming to the Sergeants' Mess as usual. The Club affair is quite small.'

I went ahead. At nine o'clock that evening there were between fifty and a hundred men standing round the dance floor – and exactly four women. The Commandant was there with Mrs Newey, but she, though smiling and genial as always, had recently been in hospital and could not dance. There was an Indian major, a charming Muslim, so westernised that he had brought his even more charming wife, but her emancipation had not yet extended to the learning of ballroom dances. From the leave-centre there were two Eurasian girls, privates in the Indian A.T.S. There was emphatically nothing wrong with *them*, they looked physically fit and unhampered by the taboos of religion, but what were two among so many? And what New Year's Eve dance ever ended before midnight?

It was an appalling situation. Everybody rose to it with the most wonderful good humour. One of the sergeants was a member of the Magic Circle. With practically no props save a pack of ordinary playing-cards he put on an impromptu display which kept the whole company enthralled for the next half-hour, while I tried to collect my whirling thoughts and put my emotions into cold storage for a more convenient time. When the conjuring ran out, we served the refreshments earlier than planned. Then we played the sort of Christmas party games we had organised for the schoolgirls a few days before. The Muslim major and his wife cavorted with the best of us. Pausing for breath, I glanced at my watch and saw with relief that it was eleven o'clock. The last hour was easy. We had only to gather round the piano and sing all the carols anyone could remember. The mess servants stood beaming in the doorway, listening to such incomprehensible western melodies as 'Silent Night' and 'Good King Wenceslas'. At least they could scarcely have seemed odder than the wild posturings and gyrations, tugs-of-war and rushings to and fro, to which the sahibs' Christian faith had impelled them earlier in the evening.

So 1946 came in, after all, with 'Auld Lang Syne' and a warm friendly feeling that embraced everyone present. I for one, though, was in no mood to propose the toast to all our 'Absent Friends'.

Fortunately, on 2 January, I started a month's leave, and was able to get right away from the station and all its pettiness.

It was entirely characteristic of Colonel Newey that he wanted all of us temporary soldiers to get leave and see more of his beloved India. Though January was not the ideal month, he advised me to make sure of it.

From boyhood, when I had borrowed from the Nottingham Public Library a book with particularly alluring watercolour illustrations, I had nourished an ambition to see for myself what I had termed, in a youthful sonnet:

The flush of rhododendrons in Kashmir. . . .

But Kashmir proved inaccessible at this season, and, as I was determined to get a glimpse of the Himalayas at some point, I settled for Darjeeling at the eastern end. Even this, one of the regulars assured me, was crazy. Everything at Darjeeling would be shut. I should never see the snows. They would be blanketed in mist. I should merely catch pneumonia.

Newey himself did not try to dissuade me. He was only grieved that even he could not so distort the regulations as to show me all of India he wanted me to see. The Chief Clerk was adamant. 'I'm sorry, Trease,' said Newey, handing me my free railway-warrant, 'Mr Gaddi says you can't possibly travel back via Delhi and Agra. Such a pity you'll have to miss the Red Fort and the Taj Mahal.'

I went down in the bus to Pipariya and boarded the Calcutta Mail from which I had stepped down five months earlier. This time I travelled in the relative comfort of second class. There was no corridor. Meal-times were signalled at the appropriate stopping-place, one walked forward to the dining-car and returned to it at some subsequent station. It was a day and a night's run to Calcutta. As we entered Bengal the country assumed a greater luxuriance. Palms and banana-trees clustered densely round green pools.

Calcutta, I recorded in my notebook, was 'faintly frightening'. The endless stream of faces pouring across the Howrah Bridge brought home to me, as nothing had before, the appalling magnitude of the population problem. I remembered one of Newey's rhetorical dicta, 'If the Indians really want the British to leave, they only need to throw one stone each.' In Bombay you still had the feeling that the West was uppermost. Here there was veiled hatred, contempt, sullenness, weariness, wildness. I never forgot that flow of faces meeting me as I walked across the bridge.

I stayed several days with an old schoolfriend, Bruce Trinder, in the prosperous residential area of Alipore. He was a big man in insurance. With three other bachelors he lived in a 'chum-mery', sharing a pleasant house and garden and a well-trained staff of servants. Bruce, though no left-winger, was obviously sympathetic to Indian aspirations. During my visit he invited to dinner the daughter of a famous Congress leader and her cousin, a student, son of a High Court judge and himself a fervid, idealistic Communist of the pattern I had met in England about 1931. Both these young people were positive that India's troubles were all due to Britain. We were even blamed for the backward farming methods. I was assured that religion was *not* such a dividing force in Indian life, and that Congress and the Muslim League would soon link up when the British had gone. This seemed to me very unconvincing.

But the next day, after Bruce had taken me as his guest into the Saturday Club ('Europeans only'), I felt a sympathetic reaction towards my late dinner-companions. Perhaps the worst of the 'Quit India' campaign from England's point of view would be the return home of some of the English.

One morning, starting out from Bruce's house, I hailed a rickshaw and told the man to take me into the city. To visit Calcutta without riding in a rickshaw seemed as serious an omission as seeing Venice without ever stepping into a gondola. But after a few minutes of bowling along the road with that wizened little man in front of me, padding along between the shafts on his bare grey dusty feet, I felt the shame rising inside me until I was almost choked. He trotted on. I could bear it no longer. No able-bodied man ought to sit enthroned as I was, with a fellow human being pulling him. He stopped for the traffic. I called out, and he looked round, breathless and beaded with sweat, his narrow chest heaving convulsively. I got down and paid him off. I could not have ridden another yard. Never more than in that episode did I feel the painful guilt I had always expected to feel when I came face to face with the poverty of India.

I was thankful to leave that instructive, appalling city. After four days I caught the Darjeeling Mail and rumbled northwards through the night. I woke early, let down the shutter on the east side of the compartment, and saw a superb crimson dawn silhouetting the palms and gleaming on the long streak of the Mahanady river. In front, a dim grey line could only be the foothills of my dreamed-of Himalayas. Remembering the dismal warnings that I should see nothing but fog in January, I said to myself exultantly: 'Well, I've seen this much, and nothing can take it away!' I was ever one to be thankful for small mercies, probably too modest in my expectations from life generally. And then, as I wrote to Marian that evening:

the incredible, beautiful thing happened: high over the foot-hills, floating in the sky, a long range of snow peaks, looking like pink marble! *Could* it be? I consulted the panoramic photo in my guide-book, checked off each peak and dip and crenellation. Yes – it *was*, it couldn't be anything else! Kinchinjunga, the third highest peak in the world. It was terrific. And I'd seen it straight off, just like that.

At Siliguri one had to leave the Calcutta express and change to the narrow-gauge line that curved and zigzagged up the steep foothills to Darjeeling, over seven thousand feet above sea-level. I was scribbling hard in my notebook. I had no idea of ever writing a book about India but it had become a habit to record impressions everywhere. Eventually that morning's notes gave me half a chapter for *The Young Traveller in India and Pakistan*. The toy railway climbed through the tea-plantations. Flaming spear-blades of poinsettia stood out against the green. At Kurseong the train ran through the street. One could stare straight into the open shops and even buy things during one of the frequent halts. But I was most struck by the delightful children, so much better clad, less whining, than at Pachmarhi. They bowled hoops down the steep roads where, if the hoop swerved, it toppled not into a kerb but over a precipitous hillside. They ran, like English boys, along low wall-tops, but here again the drop the other side was hundreds of feet. They threw paper darts and made paper propellors which twirled gaily on the end of sticks. They fenced with twigs, they too saw a forked stick as a potential catapult, they flew kites which sailed bravely out over the abyss, and from a bit of board and some cotton-reels they made themselves a little trolley car which rode gaily down the hills.

It was the dead season at Darjeeling, as I had been fairly warned. Most of the big hotels and many of the shops were shut. Luckily, I had made friends on the train with some airmen on leave from Burma. They came round to look me up in the comfortable but empty Indian hotel where I had made an advance booking, and, appalled by my solitary state, insisted that I transfer to their own guesthouse. This was run by a loquacious old Scotswoman, who was 'Ma' to everyone from the first five minutes. Ma presided at a table of perhaps a dozen of us, all the others in Air Force blue. She had a Gurkha cook who produced the most ferocious curry that has ever seared my stomach-lining. Afterwards, for relief, there were always plenty of the Sikkim oranges that glowed like lamps on every stall in the town. And finger-bowls. Ma was particular about finger-bowls. Meals were cheerful, often uproarious occasions. Ma's establishment was just the place I needed at that time.

The weather, contrary to those gloomy prophecies, was clear. Each morning, when the bearer brought in my early tea and swished back the curtains, I saw Kinchinjunga framed in the window. It took me some days to adjust my angle of sight, and to remember that, though I was seven thousand feet up, Kinchinjunga was another twenty-one thousand. At first glance I would conclude, disappointedly, that the mountain had retired at last into the clouds. Then I would realise that I was directing my gaze at a broad swathe of mist that was no more than a sash round the giant's middle. It was a question of tilting one's head up, up, and up again, till one saw the upper heights, glittering like frozen honey in the morning sunshine, at a point in the sky where only the heavenly bodies properly belonged. For three weeks my beloved Kinchinjunga was constantly in view, hung like a backcloth behind the terraced town, ever changing with the light. The spell never weakened. Writing home on my last evening, I mentioned 'a longish stroll to see the sunset, with Kinchinjunga pale and pink and ethereal in the northern distance'. That distance was forty-five miles.

An early-morning trek to catch a glimpse of Everest, an insignificant tip, barely distinguishable across the mountains between, was mere anticlimax. Rather more satisfying was a visit, partly on foot, partly by taxi, to the border of Nepal. Eight of us went. Nepal, in those pre-hippy days, had the allure of a forbidden country, only less inaccessible than Tibet. The frontier in itself proved unromantic. There were no sentries, no Customs. The road simply ran through a gap in a wall which, with the grey mist for once cutting out all distant views, could easily have been in Yorkshire. No one challenged us as we walked through, anxious as children to boast that we had 'set foot in' Nepal. Desolate though the spot seemed, urchins materialised immediately, offering to sell us Nepalese coins for Indian. As their rate of exchange gave them something like six hundred per cent profit, they were clearly – for all the fluttering prayer-flags and revolving prayer-wheels of that exotic region – not entirely immune from materialism.

Even in a sleepy, out-of-season hill-station like Darjeeling there were echoes of the political unrest convulsing the cities. Congress was celebrating the birthday of Subhas Chandra Bose, their one-time president who had fled during the war to join the Japanese. I met a small procession carrying his portrait (he had been killed in an air crash in Japan) and the marchers, seeing my uniform, broke at once into a shrill chant of 'Quit India!' How to explain to them that it was the one thing I was most anxious to do?

That anxiety, I found when I got back to Pachmarhi, was shared by the whole of the Sergeants' Mess, where the numbers were temporarily swollen by dozens of other instructors, all furious at being kept in India, doing nothing, though their education authorities at home were crying out for their services.

I could understand that, remembering Jocelyn in her grossly under-staffed school at Abingdon.

There was a feeling in the Mess, however ill-founded, that the Labour Government was deliberately slowing down the release of the troops, to avoid the trouble that had followed the rapid demobilisation of 1919. Our misgivings were heightened by the newspapers, reporting questions and answers in Parliament. Late in February I was writing home:

> I hope Isaacs' latest demob statement hasn't made you too unhappy. . . . The *News Chronicle* cutting caused a great outcry. . . . The whole extra half-million has been assigned to Navy, Air Force – and Class B. . . . The Govt. has completely betrayed us, partly to placate the rebellious Air Force, partly to give industry the Class B men in huge numbers. . . . If we were almost anywhere else (e.g. Germany or Italy) we should have had a sit-down strike by now, small as our numbers are. In view of the present volcanic situation in India, our hands are tied. . . . This isn't very suitable reading for a birthday letter, darling, but I want you to know that we all feel the same here.

We did indeed. A day or two earlier – contemptuous of King's Regulations, for we were none of us regulars and at this late stage of our service we cared about as much for military law as we did for the law of Islam – we had held a meeting and passed a unanimous resolution, which I was to take to the Commandant. Tempers were high and the mood desperate. We retained just enough prudence to avoid the sort of downright phrasing that would have come most natural to us as free men and citizens in what we stubbornly regarded still as 'real' life. We knew we could not 'protest', let alone 'demand'. We merely 'requested' that our feelings be made known to higher authority. And our feelings were of deep regret that the latest statement in Parliament would inevitably have an adverse effect upon the troops' morale.

It sounds mild enough to modern ears. But if I had handed Newey a parcel-bomb I could scarcely have shaken him more. After he had slept, or tried to sleep, on it, he summoned me to his office. There was the usual furtive check to ensure that neither Mr Gaddi nor any of his clerks was concealed behind the arras. Then, with portentous solemnity, he declared his personal sympathy with our feelings. 'But – ' and the hand went up that would have stilled the murmurs of even the *Bounty*'s crew, at least for a moment, 'believe me, Trease, I *dare* not forward that document to Jubbulpore. If I could be sure it would be opened only by a British officer. . . . ' Again the well-timed pause, the frank man-to-man stare, stern but friendly – he would have been God's own gift to any political party in the television era. 'But I cannot be sure. And that document must not be seen by any Indian.' Quick glance round to make sure that Mr Gaddi had not crept in, disguised as a spider. 'It would be misunderstood, Trease. Garbled. And the least rumour of disaffection in any British unit. . . . Once the rumour started. . . .' He shuddered. I shuddered in respectful sympathy. 'I will do my best, Trease. Tell them, I will find ways to convey their views. But I dare not do exactly what they ask.'

With that, for the time being, we had to be content. It was easy to mutter 'soft soap', hard to see what more we could do, beyond stirring up sympathetic M.P.s in England.

Some of my news from home was more cheering. Marian had heard one of my short stories broadcast and assured me it had been done well. Nan Macdonald had now accepted four, and wrote that she was preparing a full-length dramatisation of *The Grey Adventurer*, previously heard only in extracts in the Schools programme. She would put it on in the summer, so I might after all get back in time to hear it myself. This serial proved to be the first of many of mine that the B.B.C. would broadcast throughout the next decade, until the widely lamented and controversial dropping of Children's Hour. My letters back to Marian were full of plans for books and plays.

Despite my eagerness to get home, I could still respond to the Indian scene around me. At that season the trees were in full blossom, very beautiful against the pale blue skies. There were red silk cotton-trees, big and gnarled as oaks, leafless as almond-trees but covered with great crimson flowers, and there were the smaller, graceful jacarandas, with feathery leaves and what looked like immense clusters of bluebells on their branches.

The sunsets were great blazes of gold, peach and apricot behind the fantastic crags. The night landscapes were brilliant black and silver under the full moon.

The school had a day off for the Hindu festival of Holi. I stayed in and got on with my own writing, for the chief feature of Holi seemed to be the squirting of coloured water over the clothing of passers-by. I could hear the drums and the shouting in the bazaar. There seemed to be drums and shouting most days, and almost every evening. The passion for hubbub was insatiable.

Holi fell in mid-March, on the exact day I completed four years' military service. A week or two later Newey swept into the building where I was working and greeted me with regal geniality.

'Good news for you! A message has just come through. Some extra shipping available unexpectedly. Your release group is to stand by, ahead of time.'

The delicious, delirious preliminaries began. The handing over to my successor, the medical formalities, the penning of the Commandant's eulogy . . . but, alas, 'delirious' came all too near being literally true. I was still in the midst of preparations when I was stricken down by what, I assured my solicitous bearer and neighbours, was only one of the severe feverish colds to which I was subject in England. They were not convinced. An ambulance came rolling across the grass and pulled up at my verandah. I was taken to the little military hospital a short distance away, where it was confirmed that I had malaria.

It was not, I fancy, a very serious case. I felt weak and ill, but even at the time I was conscious that my symptoms lacked the drama I should have expected from novels and films. My chief worry, which hardly helped to bring down my temperature, was that I should miss the boat. If that 'unexpected extra shipping' went without me, should I lose all benefit, and slip down the queue to some position of greater disadvantage than ever? In the Army one never knew.

All was well. The movement order did not arrive until I was out of hospital. Farewells were said. Newey seemed really sorry. To my surprise, he wrote to me some time afterwards, when he was a staff officer at Scottish Command, and we kept up a correspondence until he died. I was sorry that we never met again. He had that lovable, larger-than-life quality of the old actor-managers.

Ginger Whiskers gripped my hand. Little Flit-Wallah hung a garland round my neck. My last farewell was to Dhannu, my bearer, who rode down to Pipariya behind me in the bus, and stood guard over my kit, bulging with all the family presents I could cram in, while I lunched in the dak bungalow and waited for the train. That lunch was almost the only food I could get before I reached the transit camp at the legendary Deolali, some twenty-four hours later.

Conditions there were primitive. Lines of tents on a pancake-flat plain, a hot dusty wind, leaden skies, thunder rumbling round the distant knobbly hills. . . . There was an Education Sergeant I knew, running gramophone recitals every morning. Sixty or seventy of us would sit round, stripped to the waist, sweating copiously, enjoying Bach, Handel and Haydn. At other times we were lectured on the problems of readjustment to Civvy Street. There were hints that it would be unreasonably optimistic to expect fidelity in every wife. A blind eye might be better than too violent a reaction. Not every wife was a Penelope. Not every returning warrior should emulate Odysseus. There were informative talks on careers and training schemes. I sat there with gunners, infantrymen, sappers, signalmen. Apart from my cap-badge and shoulder-titles I felt that I was out of Army Education, except as a passive recipient in these closing days. I was a body, animate admittedly, awaiting shipment home.

After a few days we went, sailing from Bombay in a Canadian Pacific liner, the *Empress of Australia*. We did not mind this time being packed like cattle, and at least we had airier sleeping-quarters in what had once been a saloon opening upon an upper deck. But on the homeward voyage there were no appetising, steward-served lunches and dinners for the warrant officers. Most of the day one seemed to be in a queue along some sun-scorched rail, clutching one's mug for tea or one's plate for a solid meal.

In such a queue I talked with a stranger, an artist in civil life. His face lit up as he spoke of getting back to his drawing-board again. I knew just how he felt. We all shared a longing to be home, most, with imaginable exceptions, were counting the days to reunion with their families. But, having said that, the majority thought in terms of holidays, sport, getting back to the lads and the local. The artist and I speculated wryly whether we were really the only two, out of the five thousand crammed into that vessel, who were eager to resume work, the 'real' work with meaning, from which the war had debarred us for so long. If so, it was a sad commentary on modern life.

At Liverpool again, as at Bombay, there was only one berth big enough for us. Again it was occupied. Again we endured forty-eight hours of frustration, this time lying in the Mersey, staring foolishly across at the Liver Buildings, excluded from our own country by a narrow strip of water.

At last, on Friday, we were able to dock, stream down the gangways and pack the waiting trains. My own draft was bound for the Guildford release-centre. Our train ran non-stop across the Midlands, on that sunny day poignantly lovely with unfurling foliage and blossom. The station name-boards, removed during the invasion scare six years earlier, had not yet been replaced. It was hard to tell just where we were, but, as I began to pick up clues, I realised that we should pass through Oxford and Radley. I scribbled a note to Marian, saying I hoped to be home the next evening, and superscribed it with a word of explanation and appeal to anyone who picked it up. I weighted it with an old paybook cover and threw it on to the deserted platform at Radley as we thundered through. Within an hour or two it was delivered to our house a mile away.

I slept my last night in an army bed at Tilehurst, outside Reading. To this day, as I flash through Tilehurst station on my way home from Paddington, the name is as emotive as Adlestrop was to Edward Thomas, and with more obvious reason.

Saturday was hectic. By army truck and train we were hustled from place to place, miles apart, for the complex process of turning us back from soldiers into civilians could not apparently be performed in a single depot, even with our most eager co-operation. By mid-afternoon we had still to reach the last square in this mad game, the civilian clothing centre where we should be given our 'demob suit', hat, shoes, macintosh, and the rest of the outfit. Our grumbling and ghoulish truck-driver assured us that by now the place would have shut for the week-end. I had a nightmare vision of being trapped, half in and half out of the military machine, until Monday.

It was not so. The clothing centre was open. We made our choice hastily, not too fastidious about colour and fit. With two or three others who, like myself, had dumped their private possessions in the luggage office at Reading that morning, I shared a taxi and raced across country to catch the Oxford train.

An hour later I was dragging out my black tin box and the rest of my baggage on to the platform at Radley. As I straightened up I heard the clatter of footsteps on the footbridge. I must have looked yellower than any Chinese, for I was still taking mepacrin for my recent malaria, but Marian and Jocelyn knew me all right. I was home.

CHAPTER TWELVE

'Soldier from the Wars Returning'

EVEN pushing a lawn-mower was, for the time being, a joy. For months I had dreamed of the scent of English grass, new-cut and juicy. Conversely, even today, there is a stretch of road near my home in Herefordshire where all India rushes back at me on a hot summer day. A neighbour's evergreen hedge runs along the top of a retaining wall, shoulder-high. The soil at its roots is always dry. A wave of blended odours comes to my nostrils – pungent foliage, sun-baked stone, and above all the dusty earth that never tastes water. For those fifty paces I am walking in India.

It was sweet to be back in the little house looking across the young corn towards Radley. About Abingdon I had not much sentiment. We had often considered alternatives. Would a flat in Oxford be better? The bigger town would be more stimulating, but would it be any friendlier? I had no illusions about university society. It was a closed world to outsiders – and I was very much an outsider, with only the vestigial link of my Union life-membership. I found the Union handy as a club, I used its restaurant and library, but it was not a place where one made friends or even exchanged a word.

For the time being, any plan to move must be deferred. To be back with my family – anywhere – a free man, a civilian, was sufficient delight. And to re-establish myself as a writer was my immediate concern.

It was almost thirteen years since I had burnt my boats. A general does that for a purpose: now he must hold his beachhead and advance – or surrender. It had taken me six years to establish a precarious foothold. Another seven years later, thanks to the war, I was almost back to square one, the boats long burnt, the beachhead still to win.

Only in one sector, in children's literature, had I won a little ground. That very month, unknown to me, a New Zealand librarian named Dorothy Neal White was completing her critical survey, *About Books for Children*, writing of my work with unusual insight and over-generously bracketing my name with Arthur Ransome's for 'popularity'. My sales would not have supported her judgement, but Blackwell had certainly kept my books on the market, despite war shortages, and I knew that this was where I must concentrate my efforts for the moment, with no hazardous sorties into the theatre or adult fiction.

For nine weeks longer I was theoretically a soldier on leave, with full pay and allowances. Men with jobs to go to might treat that period as the longest holiday of their lives. I dared not. I knew I must get busy at once. Those nine weeks represented the only subsidised writing time I had ever had or was likely to have. By the second week I was deep into the next book.

The theme had been waiting long enough. The very last idea entered in my notebook before I got my call-up papers – it was dated 2 March 1942 – ran thus: 'Plot for Renaissance story – scholar steals unique Greek MS from remote, dog-in-the-manger European monastery, so that it can be printed and translated, and given to the world.' During my last months in India the idea had begun to develop in my mind. Erasmus, Aldus Manutius and his Venetian printing-press, selfish aristocratic collectors and their unscrupulous agents ransacking remote libraries for unique classical manuscripts, only to hoard them in equally inaccessible palaces. . . . The essential conflict was there, the conflict between people and privilege, with Manutius and his popular editions to pit against wicked dukes and their minions. And there was the treasure-hunt, one of the basic half-dozen plots in children's fiction.

In writing so many stories, I have been forced to use that theme several times, though always trying to vary it and minimise the material incentive. In *The Secret Fiord* the 'treasure' is a lost father, an English mason adrift in the wilds of medieval Norway, and in *Word to Caesar* it is the evidence needed to rehabilitate a political exile. In *The Gates of Bannerdale* a perceptive reader will see that it is not really the Oxford college silver, hidden since the Civil War, but the establishment of historical truth after three centuries of injustice to the dead.

By the time I left Pachmarhi the new story was fairly bubbling in my head, but I was frustrated by lack of detailed knowledge on Aldus Manutius. Research was becoming more and more important to me, though I wince now to remember how superficial it was. Those useful volumes that now fill my study, the general books on the 'everyday life' of this epoch and that, the specialised tomes on costume and coins, ships, schools, stage-coaches and sex-life, were either still unpublished or beyond my purse. I had never seen Venice. It would be many years yet before I could follow the imagined route of my characters, sailing down the Dalmatian coast and clambering up the fabled battlements of Ragusa.

As so often, the local library had to suffice. Abingdon, with remarkable speed, got me the only traceable book on Manutius, in French. Another book, on travel in modern Yugoslavia, had to supply the background for my mountain monastery. The essential story had been bottled inside me for months. Now it poppled out like champagne.

The writing of that 241-page book occupied five weeks, interrupted by a fortnight's family holiday on the Cornish coast. Jocelyn was a good walker now. A mile for each year of her age seemed a fair distance. We followed the coast path from Looe to Polperro. Already the beach defences in the lonely inlets were rusting into history. We explored the Seaton valley, our way ribboning between yellow flags and foxgloves, wild roses and ragged robin, cow parsley and elder, and silver birches with great blobs of velvety green-brown lichen. We found a watermill working at Hessenford, with pearly strings dripping from the wheel. We met a mountainous stallion on his rounds, stamping and rolling his eyes beside the telephone kiosk, while a bandy-legged little stud-groom held his halter in one hand and tried with the other to ring some distant farm. It was good to step back into this timeless rural world. But it was good too to return to my desk and polish off the book. By the time my army pay ceased I had finished the story.

With the continuing paper shortage and the general back-log in publishing, it would be another year before Blackwell could bring out *Trumpets in the West*, so we had agreed amicably that I should be free to find a London publisher for this other book. It might be a good thing for all concerned, since a London firm would have bigger resources for publicity and marketing, and all my work would benefit indirectly as my name became better known. My first choice was Jonathan Cape, whose promotion of Arthur Ransome seemed to mark a new development in juvenile literature – treating it as though it mattered. This was my explanation to Cape himself, when he summoned me to Bedford Square a couple of months later and asked me why I had picked on his company. 'Oh, Ransome,' he said, 'of course he just discovered a formula and now anybody can copy it.' I was privately shocked by this. Though I had sometimes felt the idolatry of Ransome excessive, it seemed a rather disloyal comment from a publisher who had made a lot of money out of his work.

'Now, your book,' said Cape briskly, and my heart came into my mouth. 'I would gladly publish it, but' – my heart plummeted – 'I should have to hold it back for a couple of years, and you can't starve while the grass grows. You want a publisher with plenty of paper.'

'How do I find one?' I asked glumly.

'There are two publishers with plenty of paper at this moment. Go to Miss Z at Collins – or to Lovat Dickson at Macmillan's. I know them both well. Tell them from me that this is a book I would gladly publish if I had the paper, but I haven't.'

I was out in Bedford Square, the package of typescript in my hand. Curiously enough, the name of Miss Z – which now completely eludes me – was the more familiar at that time. I rang her office. She was away on holiday. So, by one of the happiest accidents in my life, I turned my steps towards Macmillan, then in a dingy little side-street running down from Leicester Square.

There was nothing dingy about their offices. A panelled entrance hall led to a broad, shallow staircase. There were photographs of Macmillan authors . . . Kipling, Eric Linklater, Storm Jameson, Charles Morgan . . . would my own be ever among them? It would – but I was not allowed to bank on the prospect that day.

I was granted an audience. Lovat Dickson towered above me. He looked very distinguished. 'I suppose you realise', he said severely, 'that Macmillan's demand a *very* high standard in their children's books? We were the original publishers of Lewis Carroll.'

'I don't delude myself that I'm another Lewis Carroll,' I said as firmly as I could. 'All I wanted to ask you was this: will *you* keep my book another couple of months and then say you like it but haven't any paper?'

'No,' he said. 'I can promise you. If we like your book we can certainly publish it.'

His acceptance came two weeks later. There remained only the punctilious clearance with Blackwell. Macmillan did not poach. By the end of October the agreement was signed and a long happy relationship had begun. A children's writer, if versatile and prolific, is almost compelled to use more than one publisher, but he can plan his output so as to keep everyone happy. There need be no desertions, no disloyalties. Literary monogamy may be impracticable, but a kind of polygamous fidelity, at least in the author–publisher relationship, works surprisingly well.

Macmillan had only one other query. My original title, *The Hills of Svana*, might trouble some children as being awkward to pronounce. Rather too hastily I changed my imaginary 'Svana' to 'Varna', forgetting that there was a real Varna of some importance in Bulgaria and thus creating a slight geographical ambiguity which it was too late afterwards to correct. In America the publishers' habitual passion for changing titles had, for once, the fortunate result of altering this one to *The Shadow of the Hawk*. In later years, reasonably enough, they found *Mist Over Athelney* too obscure and asked me to change it to *Escape to King Alfred*. *Thunder of Valmy* became *Victory at Valmy*, which they said, in a revealing phrase, conveyed to American readers the idea of 'positive and successful action'. My *Crown of Violet*, though inspired by Pindar, would never do. No red-blooded American boy would open a book with a flower in the title. So this story came out in New

York as *Web of Traitors*, and I always had a sneaking fear that its initial sales owed something to a possible confusion with the anti-Communist witch-hunt then being conducted by Senator McCarthy.

In the end even Macmillan took two years to publish *The Hills of Varna*. Meanwhile, to hold my beachhead, I had to busy myself in other ways.

I had dreamed of work and I could scarcely complain if the dream was now fulfilled – and occupied almost every waking hour. It must have been dull for Marian, as the typewriter clicked monotonously on, or, like some primeval hunter, I left her for long days to hunt for our livelihood. Lecture-invitations came from the National Book League and other sources. I could not afford to miss a guinea or a chance to make my books known. Small wonder that, turning the pages of my 1947 diary, I am reminded of little but trains and lecture-halls and carafes of cold water.

Jan. 14, Ramsgate Arts Society, 'An Author Under the Soviets'. . . . Jan. 22, dined at Balliol and lectured, 'Is Russia Rationalist?' . . . Jan. 26, stay with Dudley Collard, Manchester Street, en route for Barnet Book Week. 27, 28, 29, Barnet. Early dinner. Conway Hall, 7 p.m. 'India's Problem: Race or Religion?' . . . Feb. 4, Tottenham Book Week, 1.45 and 2.45, 'A Book is Born'. Dined Norman Swallow at Authors' Club.

Swallow had not then begun his brilliant career in television, which itself had only just restarted after the war. He was the B.B.C.'s North Regional Features Producer at Manchester, where, besides my Children's Hour connection, I was selling an occasional short story for adult listeners. As the Regions were not supposed to poach on each other's territory, a certain protocol had to be observed. Producers could accept scripts, whatever their subject-matter, from writers who lived or had been born in, their region. Alternatively, if the subject-matter was local, the writer need not be. There was another slight difficulty in that I wanted to write plays, and he wanted me to, but he was not Drama Producer. We solved this by basing my plays firmly on historical facts, so that they had a demonstrable documentary flavour, though the technique was purely dramatic. This work was some consolation for my frustration in the theatre itself.

The idea we discussed that night over dinner was the double life of Friedrich Engels, who combined membership of the Manchester Cotton Exchange and riding to fox-hounds (privately justified as practice for leading the cavalry when the Communist revolution came) with his collaboration with Marx and his illicit love-life with an Irish immigrant. *Mr Engels of Manchester 'Change* was successfully broadcast a few months later. 'We got by with it just in time,' Norman told me with a grin, for the increasing public disenchantment with Russia made Marxism a sensitive subject with the B.B.C. Our subsequent plays were less controversial. *Countess Anne* was inspired by that forthright Jacobean character, Anne Clifford, and *The Real Mr Ryecroft* traced the parallels between Gissing's own life and that of his fictitious man of letters. During this period the regional convention enabled me to write biographical plays on Raleigh and Irving for Desmond Hawkins at the Bristol studios.

All this had to be fitted in with writing books – five in two years – and the continual lecture journeys. The 1947 diary goes on: 'Feb. 12, Nottingham Writers' Club, 'A Play is Born'. Mar. 4, Mitcham Book Week, 2 talks, 'A Book is Born'. Mar. 11, Hornsey Book Week, 'A Book is Born'. Conway Hall, 7 p.m. 'What Shall Our Children Read?' Mar. 15, Soviet reception.'

This function was in honour of some visiting deputies. I attended with the aim of making discreet inquiries about my current standing in Russia. Was I, as in 1935, a popular and respected, if non-Communist, foreign writer? Or had I become, without anyone mentioning it to me, a discredited Fascist jackal? It would be interesting to know. I could not continue much longer lecturing on Russia without another visit, however brief, to bring me up to date. But Soviet publishing houses not only sent no royalties abroad, they did not even ask permission to publish, notify one of the *fait accompli*, or supply the customary author's copies. At the reception I managed to buttonhole an eminent member of the Writers' Union. He made sympathetic noises and diligent notes. 'Of course, of course. . . . The matter will be looked into.' The preceding decade of blank silence was succeeded by another. Indeed, it was not until the early 1960s that I received an indirect answer to my speculations. It was a picture postcard of Red Square, sent by my friend, Antony Kamm, then visiting Moscow for the National Book League. He wrote: 'I am dining out on the score of knowing you!' It appeared that I was still very much *persona grata. Crown of Violet* was published in a school edition. *Cue for Treason, Comrades for the Charter* and *Missing from Home,* an early story of England in the Depression, shared a massive omnibus volume. Even in the Estonian language, read by barely a million people, this omnibus edition ran to 30,000 copies.

I could have used a little of that money.

Instead, I rushed to and fro across the railway map of England, grubbing for guineas. My other 1947 engagements took me to Cardiff, Cumberland, Ramsgate again, Hatfield, Luton, Wolverhampton, Birmingham, Nottingham, Newbury, and half-a-dozen different London boroughs. The total fees came to about a hundred pounds.

Voluntary organisations, with only their members' subscriptions, seldom realise that their limited funds are no logical excuse for asking authors to interrupt their work and make exhausting journeys to entertain them for a derisory fee. Somewhere I read, about this time, the trenchant advice of the veteran S. P. B. Mais. Charge a decent amount, he argued, and insist on first-class travel: *then* you will be met at the station, dined and wined, well looked after throughout, and warmly thanked for coming. Listen to their protestations of poverty, reduce your fee, and you will be treated like a dog. I recall his words inexactly, but I got his message, indelibly.

I was not Mais, however, and, though I would not work for nothing, I could not play high and mighty. Once in a while I jibbed. The Radley Women's Institute invited me to talk on children's books and as they met only a mile away I promised to go for some tiny sum. As the date drew nearer, the secretary came to see me. With obvious embarrassment the poor woman communicated her committee's new proposal: finding funds low, they wondered if I would talk for half the time at half the fee. I explained good-humouredly (I hope) that condensation was the hardest part of an author's craft. I would talk for twice the time at half the fee, if they liked, or half the time at twice the fee – but would it not be better, on the whole, to drop the idea? We agreed on that, and I gave one less lecture that year.

Local authorities too showed a laudable regard for their ratepayers' financial interests. One day I gave morning and afternoon talks in a drab Manchester suburb that fell within the Lancashire County Council's territory. The charming children's librarian apologised for our having to walk more than a mile, between lectures, to get a passable lunch in the nearest hotel. We hurried back in time to greet the local councillor who was to chair the afternoon session.

'Ye've 'ad yer dinner?' he inquired.

My hostess explained where we had been.

'Do ye'selves well, don't ye?' he said grumpily. 'Perfectly good British Restaurant round t' corner.'

British Restaurants were canteen-like survivals from the war, economical but not convivial. The price of our three-course hotel-lunch, itself still subject to war-time controls, had been three shillings and sixpence.

Over those years I could have made an anthology of chairmen and other local notables. There was the lady mayor of the London borough who, as I helped her to don her chain, remarked, 'I thought the children should have something *nice* to look at while they're listening to you.' My favourite was a member of an education committee who, over subsequent cups of tea in the head's study, came up and congratulated me with obvious surprise in his voice. 'You know I quite *enjoyed* that, Mr Trease! When I first come in this afternoon and saw you, I thought it were going to be dull!'

It was not always like that. There were stimulating encounters, all too brief, with enthusiastic teachers and librarians, articulate children, and fellow lecturers when there was an overlap in time.

My longest trip involved eight days in west Cumberland. It began with a book week at Millom, the tiny port and iron town. There was nowhere to stay, so the speakers slept at the High

Cross Inn above Broughton-in-Furness, with breath-catching views of Morecambe Bay, Black Combe, and the sharp wooded fells above the Duddon. This was Norman Nicholson country, and, during a free hour next day, I walked round to the outfitter's shop in Millom, run by his father, and tried to pay my respects to the young poet. Unhappily he was ill in bed that day, and I missed a meeting which I hoped that he too would have welcomed. For, as the local headmaster told me, almost with tears in his eyes, after my evening talk, 'Nobody has ever *come* to Millom before, nobody! You're the first.' It made the effort seem worth while.

There had been moments, earlier in that three-lecture day, when I could have wished for a little less zeal on the teachers' part. Some came from tiny single-handed schools in remote dales. To bring the children who might benefit from a book talk they had been forced to close for the day and bring the lot. As a result I faced one of the most difficult audiences of my life. Many were far too young. They sat on backless benches in a chapel with a stone floor, dangling restive feet shod in steel-tipped clogs. And they knew that there would be a film when I stopped talking. It was not easy to arouse their interest in books.

The afternoon audience made up for them. Two schoolgirls buttonholed me afterwards. 'Do you ever write school stories?'

'No,' I said. 'Haven't you got enough already? All those midnight feasts in the dorm, those secret passages and hooded figures – '

They cut me off, with grave courtesy. They didn't mean that stuff. Why didn't I write true-to-life stories, about real boys and girls, going to day-schools as nearly everybody did? No one seemed to write that sort.

Out of that five-minute conversation came, a year or two later, *No Boats on Bannermere* and eventually its four sequels, three hundred thousand words, the writing spread intermittently over nine years. I was glad I had been to Millom.

It was strange, when I left there, to be taking that west-coast line, squeezed between fells and sea, which had carried me so often to Seascale, and the Gosforth school. It would have given me a bitter-sweet satisfaction to drop in on Harecroft

Hall again, but there was no chance. The train carried me on to Maryport, where I stayed for the next few days at the educational settlement, looking across sheds and sidings to the choppy green and purple waters of the Solway. There were lectures at different places in that forsaken industrial corner of Cumberland. Whitehaven, Flimby, Broughton Moor, Dearham, Allonby . . . then a late-night departure, a midnight change at Carlisle – more emotive memories! – fitful sleep, hunched in the corner of a third-class compartment, and a 7 a.m. arrival at Euston. But I was home in good time for Jocelyn's eleventh birthday the next day.

I was now starting my second book for Macmillan, *The Secret Fiord*, set mainly in medieval Norway and dealing with the struggle against the monopolistic Hanseatic League. We had all been to Norway that August. I never wanted, if I could help it, to write another book set in a country I had not seen for myself. So we began in Bergen, exploring the old Hanseatic warehouses along the quay and learning about the special shutters that were to prove so handy for my young hero's escape. Then we went up into the mountains, the haunted troll country where my characters would continue their quest. That Norwegian trip, in the remarkable heat-wave of 1947, began a series of annual visits to various parts of Europe. Marian and I had a backlog of foreign travel to catch up on, and we wanted to make the most of the years in which Jocelyn would be young enough to stay with us.

Apart from those two weeks in Norway, I worked almost a seven-day week, never daring to relax. Besides the lectures, the radio-scripts and the books, I took on any reviewing I could get. It had to be children's literature, and there was not much critical work going in that field. The *New Statesman* gave me an occasional handful of books if I went to Great Turnstile, and by walking on to Fleet Street I might get some more from *Tribune*, then a more general magazine. Peggy Volkov, running a progressive educational monthly, the *New Era*, sent me plenty of review-copies but could pay no cash. I wrote to the famous literary weekly, *John o' London's*, offering my services and enclosing samples. I received a polite but non-committal reply, and heard no more. Then, paying one of my rare visits

to the Authors' Club, which I had joined on Basil Blackwell's
recommendation, though Whitehall was off my usual beat and
I seldom met any authors there, I sat down at the long table
laid for members lunching alone. My affable Yorkshire neighbour, a real Priestleyan character, proved to be Wilson
Midgley. We got on well from the start, he shared my love
of the Lakes, and from that day I was 'in', so far as *John o'
London's* was concerned. I was a frequent contributor until
the final issue, seven years later, when the magazine abruptly
and lamentably died under the next editor.

Though I graduated to general literature I naturally began
with children's books. Midge liked them all mentioned. I spent
whole days at the office near Covent Garden, sifting the treasure
from the trash, but making enough hasty notes on the trash
to work them into my article. About a dozen books of obvious
quality went home in my bag for careful reading.

The general standard was still deplorable. Many stories
were based on the assumptions which I had challenged when I
began writing in 1933, and Orwell had attacked seven years
later. The aristocratic bias in history, the jingoism and racial
superiority, the school-story snobbery, the class attitudes, were
all still conspicuous. It was not difficult to write lively, if
sometimes acid, reviews.

Serious criticism of children's literature was in its infancy.
Most people were surprised by the mere idea. I felt rather
pleased when, in the autumn of 1947, I managed to get the
subject included in a radio causerie called 'Books and Authors'.
It gave me only about seven minutes on the air, but it was perhaps the first seven minutes of broadcast time ever devoted to
the topic. And for me, at least, it had an important consequence.

A few days later I was talking to Peggy Volkov at the *New
Era*. Her paper was the organ of the New Education Fellow-
ship, which was also just launching an educational book club.
Vernon Mallinson, of Reading University, was the general
editor. Suitable books would be commissioned, and produced by
William Heinemann, whose imprint would be carried on a
general edition for sale to non-members.

'Why not write us a book *on* children's books?' Peggy
Volkov suggested.

I was taken aback. Normally I was ready to have a go at anything, but I hesitated. 'Is there a whole book *in* it?' I said. 'I've talked for seven minutes on the B.B.C. – I once wrote twelve hundred words for a Sunday newspaper – but a whole *book*?'

'We can help,' she said. 'We can give you introductions, perhaps suggest lines of inquiry. Do think about it.'

I thought, and the book began to take shape. Because it was based on my original contention, that we had dangerously ignored the effects of children's leisure-time reading, I called it *Tales Out of School*.

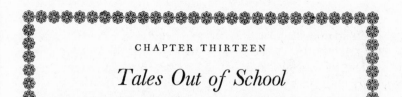

CHAPTER THIRTEEN

Tales Out of School

WRITING a critical survey of juvenile fiction was rather a risky adventure in 1948. It meant an advance into a luxuriant jungle without maps. And when the explorer was not an impartial librarian or educationist, but himself an active author, criticising his contemporaries, he was vulnerable to attack from all sides. Some of the arrows would be venomous.

'Without maps,' I said. There was admittedly Harvey Darton's monumental volume, *Children's Books in England: Five Centuries of Social Life*, then out of print and stopping short of my own period. That, supplemented with individual biographies of people like Ballantyne, gave me adequate material about the past, though I did not discover until too late Roger Lancelyn Green's *Tellers of Tales*. In any case its original 1946 edition was quite different from his subsequent revision, and was then meant 'for young readers in their early teens'. It excluded all authors still alive.

The past was not my main concern. Indeed I was, and still am, impatient of the sentimental nostalgia that overwhelms most adults when children's books are mentioned. 'Beatrix Potter!' they coo. 'E. Nesbit! Mrs Ewing!' Try to discuss contemporary writing and the coos turn to yawns.

I meant to give the past its place in the book. I was going to trace the winding course of each genre from its original spring. The school story, for example, a unique English phenomenon, sprang from *Tom Brown's Schooldays*, quickly received *Eric* as a tributary, grew in volume with the books of Talbot Baines Reed, was given a new twist by *Stalky and Co.*, and after almost a century was petering out in the sand. The adventure story, the historical novel, fantasy, talking animals, space travel –

most, but not all, types of children's fiction had a comparable development spread over several generations. It was interesting, it was illuminating, it was necessary, but only as a preliminary to a study of the present and a discussion of the future.

Here the trackless jungle began. There was almost no serious criticism of contemporary children's literature in Britain. There were a few pioneers who cared. Kathleen Lines, Eileen Colwell and Eleanor Graham were at work, but they had not written books. It was only from about 1960 onwards, still twelve years and more away, that the main body of critics moved into action, straddling the columns of the quality newspapers with their reviews and producing at last a respectable body of general criticism in book form. Margery Fisher, Naomi Lewis, Margaret Meek, Brian Alderson, Marcus Crouch, John Rowe Townsend and Edward Blishen were all still to come. I had to scour the world for such relevant scraps of material as I could find. Paul Hazard in France (but writing of English books), Jeanne Cappe in Belgium, Anne Carroll Moore in America, Dorothy Neal White in New Zealand, an international report from Geneva – such were the only printed sources I had to help me.

There were advantages. Perhaps too much literary criticism is spun out of earlier critics' publications. I was forced to concentrate on the raw material, the children's books themselves.

My desk became untidier than ever. I had no study in the little house at Abingdon. I dreamed of possessing one some day, and I can well believe that my family dreamed of it with equal longing. I had my desk in a corner of the living-room. Luckily I was not one to burn the midnight oil. I worked pretty regularly through the mornings and afternoons, and the typewriter was usually silent by the time Jocelyn came in from school. It was not so easy at week-ends – struggling writers get into the habit of a seven-day week – or during the holidays and my mother's visits. My family were marvellously patient and self-denying. But it is a strain to be continually checking household noises and restricting riotous games to the back garden when there is far more space in the front.

It must have been a welcome relief when my researches took

me into Oxford for a few hours. The red double-decker bus
passed our house on its bumbling, circuitous route through
Radley and Kennington. Many a story or other piece of writing
have I sketched in my mind as I sat in the coveted front seat
above the driver's head, enjoying the unobstructed panorama
of woods and fields and the curve of the river below Iffley
church. At the Oxford City Library I introduced myself to the
junior department, explained what I was doing, and was given
permission to browse among the children's books. This was the
simplest way to study what had been published during the last
ten or twenty years, and I used to sit there hunched up on a
child's low chair, a handful of books beside me, awkwardly
scribbling notes at a table better suited to a Japanese tea-
ceremony. For the new books I could get all the information I
needed from my own reviewing.

Soon I had drafted my chapter-headings and discussed them
with the book club's editorial committee. 'Cloak and sword',
'Midnight in the dorm', 'Tough as they come'. . . . I was
tempted to suggest 'Gymkhana and jodhpur', for the spate of
pony books for hippomaniac schoolgirls was then at its height,
with an endless series of titles like *A Pony for Jean*, *Another
Pony for Jean*, and *More Ponies for Jean*. In those days you
could have sold *Richard III* if you had given it the right
wrapper and called it *A Pony for Richard*. But in the end I had
to lump all these books together with the rest of the 'holiday'
stories that by this time were replacing the school stories of an
earlier generation.

There was a good deal of letter-writing. True to their
promise, Peggy Volkov and her colleagues gave me introductions and suggested lines of inquiry. New vistas opened up
through the jungle. My heart and the ground under me quaked
in sympathy as I sensed the danger of getting bogged down in
sociological and psychological areas that I was not equipped to
explore. If one left no stone unturned, one would find too many
odd things beneath for classification. I left it to later investi-
gators to suggest the dark underlying significance of Carroll,
Kenneth Grahame and Barrie. As for my contemporaries, it was
well to remember the law of libel.

I had some rather unrewarding correspondence with the firms

publishing comics. I was, somewhat reluctantly, including these in my study. The editorial committee were of course quite right: as I discovered later at question-time in countless lecture-rooms, when adults are not being nostalgic about children's books they are tiresomely obsessed with comics. They are naturally anxious to remain on safe, familiar ground: they remember the books they loved in their own childhood and they often cast their eyes over their children's comics, but they hate to show ignorance of the more demanding new literature they cannot be bothered to read.

So comics must be examined. I had to buy copies specially, for Jocelyn, though omnivorous in most respects, had shown no interest in them once she had passed the early *Sunny Stories* stage. By this time she was a rapid and voracious reader, ranging happily from Malcolm Saville to Naomi Mitchison's adult novels in the same weekend. I wrote to the big publishing houses and an obscure small one, endeavouring to draw from them the philosophy, if any, that lay behind their activities. Thomson of Dundee, instantly on guard, refused all information, feeling unable to discuss their 'business methods with an outside person'. Their London rival, the Amalgamated Press, granted me a long audience with two bland executives. I could not wring from them any admission that their vast influence on children's reading imposed any great responsibility or afforded any golden opportunity.

Much more productive were the approaches to some of my most famous contemporaries. In those days I knew scarcely any writers for children. The Society of Authors had not formed its sub-section, the Children's Writers' Group, which was later to bring us together to debate our common interests. Indeed, it was only in this year that I joined the Society itself, having hitherto assumed quite wrongly that it would not welcome anyone so insignificant as a children's writer. Then, finding that *Bows Against the Barons* was being pirated in France, I inquired about membership and began an association which grew ever closer and more helpful with the passing of the years, bringing countless personal friendships along with the purely professional advantages. But I should have been incredulous if anyone had told me then that, a quarter of a century later, I

should take over a chairmanship once held by men like Rider
Haggard, St John Ervine and Osbert Sitwell.

For my task in 1948 it was perhaps an advantage to know
nobody. It left the edge of criticism undulled by personal feelings
I wrote to two authors, Malcolm Saville and Kitty Barne,
whose work I admired and who both later became my friends.
I wrote also to the two foremost popular authors of the day,
Captain W. E. Johns, the creator of the ultra-British Biggles,
and Enid Blyton, so prolific that she was falsely supposed by
some to be a factory. My letters to all four were similar. The
gist, diplomatically phrased, posed the question: why, apart
from the money, did they write for children? I added that I
should assume permission to quote unless told otherwise.

All the replies were illuminating. Johns told me that, even
with the paper shortage, his books were being published at the
rate of more than a quarter of a million copies every year. He
went on:

> They appear in nearly every European language and three
> Oriental ones. Make a note that these countries are trying
> to educate their youth to the British way of life. They have
> told me so. . . . I give boys what they want, not what their
> elders and betters think they ought to read. I teach at the
> same time, under a camouflage. I teach the spirit of team-
> work, loyalty to the Crown, the Empire, and to rightful
> authority. . . . The brain of a boy is flexible, still able to
> absorb. It can be twisted in any direction. . . . Upon us, who
> cater for him at the most impressionable age of his life, rests
> a responsibility which has been perceived by at least one
> political party. To them I must give credit for working out
> that in four or five years' time these readers will be voters.
> Biggles, therefore, may have some bearing on the future of
> the country. But he will remain Biggles. He isn't interested
> in politics. He stands for something higher.

From Enid Blyton I received, by return post, six pages of
single-spaced typing which convincingly demonstrated her
genuine speed of composition and her complete self-confidence.
She wrote:

I write for children because: first, I love them and understand them, and know exactly what they want. . . . Children's
writers have definite responsibilities towards their young
public. Right should always be right, and wrong should be
wrong, the hero should be rewarded, the villain punished.

Later, for some reason, I think she regretted the help she had
given me. She was asked to serve on a brains trust, learned
that I also was invited, and made my removal a condition of
her own acceptance. She was almost incredulous, the organisers
informed me, when my invitation stood and she was unable to
sit.

My feelings about her were less emotional. I never went
along with those librarians who banned her books. I regretted
only the mediocrity of her work and its prodigious quantity,
which came between children and much better things. A little
Blyton was all right, in the early years, to help children master
the technique of reading and associate a sense of pleasure with
the printed word. The danger was only when, as too often
happened, lazy-minded children stayed with Blyton books too
long. Once, when Kitty Barne and I were joint speakers at
Guide Headquarters in London, the inevitable embarrassing
question cropped up, what did we think of Enid Blyton? Much
to my relief, Kitty Barne took that ball and sent it deftly back
across the net. 'Oh, I think the Blyton books have quite a place,'
she said with deceptive sweetness, 'for children who are not
very *old*, or not very *clever*, or not very *well*.'

It was the sheer gusto, the easy readability, of those books
that, to an uncritical public, outweighed their lack of originality
and their undistinguished style. Whether or not Enid Blyton
knew, as she claimed, exactly what children wanted, she
certainly knew how to convince them that it was what she was
giving them. At another children's gathering, in Blackwell's
bookshop, she herself was the speaker. After giving her talk,
she asked the audience what they would like her to write about
next. Suggestion after suggestion poured in. 'Note that down,
Mr So-and-so,' she instructed her escorting publisher. Finally,
she turned to the entranced young listeners and made a solemn
promise: 'All these stories will be ready in the shops for you

by next Christmas.' Over the tea-cups, a member of the staff
inquired diffidently: 'Haven't you taken on rather a lot, Miss
Blyton? That must be about twelve books you've promised
to write.' 'Oh, they're all *written*,' said the authoress. 'They're
in production.' Her literary ability was at least matched, if not
surpassed, by her business acumen.

I had to write my own book at a fair speed. It was, after all,
a bit of personal polemics, designed to open up a subject, not
to close it, so that I was under no obligation to read everything –
for which, in any case, one lifetime would have been too short.
But I had to be careful to bring no charges and make no claims
that I could not substantiate. I found it an exhilarating exercise,
very different from anything I had ever done before. What with
saeva indignatio against the numerous books I deplored, and
warm enthusiasm for good ones I had discovered and longed
to promote, there was no danger of my tiring before the job
was done.

Done it was, within six months, despite interruptions for
Book Weeks and B.B.C. commissions, a spring holiday in
Dorset and other welcome diversions. Production schedules
never regained their pre-war speed but the gaps between
delivery and publication were getting less. My book was to
come out in time for Christmas.

Incurably optimistic, I was beginning to feel a pleasurable
frisson of anticipation. This would be my first book for adults
since those two novels, stifled in infancy by the catastrophes of
1939 and 1940. The book club people, and Heinemann who
were handling the trade edition, seemed enthusiastic. The job
itself had been a joy to do, but if there were also some material
rewards in cash and credit I should not disdain them.

A visit to Cambridge in late October increased my confidence
that I had hit upon a new theme that would interest a number
of people. I was asked to speak to the Shirley Society at St
Catherine's and chose the same title for my talk as I had given
my book. I dined at high table beforehand. T. R. Henn, then
senior tutor, looked after me splendidly, and, with private
memories of my own abortive career at Oxford, I got considerable pleasure from my courteous treatment by so eminent a
scholar. Various dons made agreeable murmurs about the

novelty of my subject and I was particularly diverted by the approach, when we had crossed the court to the meeting-place, of a tall and immensely impressive figure in gown and white bands.

'You will understand and forgive me, Mr Trease, if you observe me leaving the meeting at question-time?' I am the Senior Proctor, and I have to patrol the streets.'

A year or two later I should have seen that moment as pure C. P. Snow. Just then I was conscious only of the contrast with moments at Oxford in another October in 1929.

The meeting itself was packed and went well. The quotations from bad books were received with much hilarity; the questions came thick and fast, but were strongly in sympathy with the case I had put forward. In so far as the lecture was a foretaste of my book, I left Cambridge considerably encouraged.

I could hardly wait now for publication-day. This book had taken on a very special significance for me, perhaps an exaggerated importance. My impatience was intensified by an external circumstance. Once more, as in 1938 and 1939, personal hopes were overshadowed by the international situation. It was the time of the Berlin airlift. The Russians had severed all road, rail and canal communications between West Berlin and the outside world, hoping to make the position of the British, American and French garrisons untenable. Every ton of supplies, not only for the troops but for the civilian population, had to be flown in, and every time I switched on the radio news I was braced for some report of hostile interference – even some accidental 'incident' – that would plunge us into the third world war.

In such a period it seems absurd that a writer should stop to ask himself in anguish, 'Will my book ever come out?' but writers can be very absurd. I myself was optimistic – in my calmer moments. I saw no reason for war this time, only the risk of tragic miscalculation, whereas ten years before there had been a fatalistic conviction that war with Hitler was inevitable. Still, the atmosphere was too similar to be comfortable. Would *Tales Out of School* share the fate of *Colony*?

My suspense was increased by an ordinary publishing delay. Though the book was already printed with '1948' on the title-page, it was found that it could not be bound and distributed in time for Christmas, so publication was postponed until January. We went down to spend Christmas in Dorset with Jon Evans, the friend of my Bloomsbury youth, who from the seclusion of the Isle of Purbeck still acted as literary adviser to Victor Gollancz. The festivities were punctuated with ominous news bulletins. Allied planes were being harassed in the air corridors. At any moment the real shooting might begin – and then how long before the bomb?

The Russian blockade was kept up until late in 1949, but the menace gradually ebbed before then. The book duly came out, and its reception was all I had hoped for. Not only did it win the judicious approval of the educational journals but it got a three-column spread in the *Times Literary Supplement* and praise from such critics as Edward Shanks and Walter Allen. Not least helpful was John Betjeman's long review in the *Daily Herald*: 'As soon as I started it, I was fascinated and made to laugh out loud.' That was what it needed, to get the wider public reading it. Heinemann were soon reprinting, and then bringing out a cheap edition.

The writing of this book affected my life in various ways. One was the change in the nature of my lecturing. Hitherto, with a few exceptions, my invitations had been to talk to children either in schools or in public libraries. I kept up that work, for the contact with boys and girls was always so stimulating, but the publication of *Tales Out of School* produced a spate of requests from adult organisations. Birmingham University, the Cumberland County Teachers' Association, the London Association of English Teachers, the Nottingham Education Study Society, the Nottingham Institute of Education, the Youth Section of the Library Association – suddenly, everyone decided that children's literature was a matter worth serious consideration.

It is tempting to think, too, that the book affected the writing and publishing of children's books in the decade that followed. It should have done to judge from the letters I received, not only from fellow-authors but from editors, teachers and librarians who welcomed what I had said. Children's literature was, of course, ready for a great leap forward, as, following the war, younger editors and librarians with fresher notions took over the places of their elders. Though, to be sure, there had been precious little sign of such changes after the previous war. *Tales Out of School* coincided with an auspicious moment – it was later in 1949, for example, that Rosemary Sutcliff made her début with *The Queen Elizabeth Story*, and she was but one of a shining company of new writers who were to make the 1950s and 1960s a golden age.

When, in 1964, I was asked to revise my book, I realised with dismay and gratification how much fresh work was involved. Fifteen years had seen a transformation. A third needed completely rewriting. Scarcely a page could be left without alteration. I like to think that this need for wholesale revision was, at least in part, my own fault. I had asked for it, and, whether by coincidence or not, I had certainly got it.

CHAPTER FOURTEEN

The Beachhead Won

LIFE was not really all work in those days, though it may sound like it. I had always written fast. I had learned early to follow the original creative flash with systematic design. More gradually I had picked up the knack – and I instinctively touch wood even now as I write the words – of mastering material and anticipating pitfalls, so as not to be faulted by specialists. So, in the eight years after the war, I wrote eighteen books as well as radio scripts, articles and reviews, as well as giving countless lectures, yet there was time for living too, for travel and theatres, for visiting friends and being visited.

Often in the Army I had dreamed of the journeys we would make in Europe when it and we were free. As my army pay credit or some royalty cheque came in, I would assuage my wanderlust with naïve accountancy, naïve because I was supposing that money would keep its value. I would note that *this* amount would take us down the Danube, *this*, salted down in savings certificates, would carry us to Scandinavia. When the time came the arithmetic proved over-optimistic, but that did not matter. We were able to travel, though it meant roughing it.

I am glad that we managed it before the Mediterranean coasts were lined with concrete honeycombs and urban Europe was rebuilt in the new standardised international style. We were just in time to see a world which, if it has still not entirely disappeared, is unfamiliar to the air-lifted travelling multitudes of today. We crossed the sea in crowded, pitching steamers. We filed along rainswept railway tracks, heaved ourselves and our rucksacks into the carriages beetling above us, peered for couchette numbers, and covertly studied the strangers with whom we were to spend the night. Sometimes we travelled third class, using French family tickets, two-and-a-quarter fares for three. We wound through the mountains on branch-lines now probably no more.

We saw the straining cypresses of Provence, the red earth and pink blossom and bone-pale hills, though it meant sitting up all night on wooden seats, reaching Avignon in the chill dawn, and cowering from the mistral in a doorway on the Place du Palais until our little hotel awoke and opened its shutters to the new day. That was the low-key start to one April fortnight, in which Marian gazed her fill on her favourite post-Impressionist landscapes and Jocelyn and I saw our first great Roman monuments at Orange, Arles and the Pont du Gard. And Jocelyn learned that in France, if she strayed from our side, she would never find herself alone for long.

There were other visits to France. In Paris we stayed at a students' *pension* near the Luxembourg, where after dinner the talk seemed to flow on for ever, up and down the long table, no one rising from the hard chairs and no early hope of sleep for ourselves, since Marian and I had a room opening straight from the *salle à manger*. For the Loire châteaux we based ourselves mainly on a charming but inexpensive establishment, favoured by discriminating lorry-drivers, on the Quai du Foix at Blois. Then we moved on to an ancient riverside inn at Amboise. It was a pouring wet night, it was impossible to put one's nose outside, but we were given a splendid crackling fire in our room. Jocelyn had run out of books. To pass the time, I began to tell her, as well as I could from memory, the story of the 1914 war. She found it interesting and I had to finish it the following evening. It was the quality of her response to this, coupled with that of the boys remembered from Harecroft, that encouraged me in later years to tackle an ambitious project, the explanation of everything that had happened since 1901 in terms comprehensible, and sufficiently interesting, to adolescent readers. *This Is Your Century* was not published until 1965, but the seed was sown that night in 1950 as we sat round that open stove with its blazing logs, cosily insulated from the wet world outside.

I was avid to see Greece, and to show it to Jocelyn, who had surprised me by electing to learn Greek at Oxford High

School. I would never have pressed her – after throwing up my own Classics scholarship I was in no position to press anyone – but I was delighted by her decision. Remembering what a grind the early stages of Greek could be, I was anxious to give her an immediate glimpse of the world she would enter if she persevered. We could not immediately go to Greece; it was too far, too expensive and too unsettled with smouldering civil war. All I could do for the moment was to write her a story, *The Crown of Violet*, in which I tried to bring to life the Athens in which Aristophanes was writing his comedies and the young Plato was hanging on the words of Socrates. I dedicated the book to 'J. and her friends who chose Greek'. There were only three other girls.

It seemed a pity that I could not delay writing this story until I had seen the country myself. It meant a breach of my general resolution always, in future, to study my foreign backgrounds at first hand. In this case, however, there was something to be said for the view that classical Athens might be more accurately pictured from its own literature than from a visit to the modern city with its traffic, industrialisation and outspreading suburbs.

Still, the determination to see Greece did not weaken, and the next spring, just as the book was published, we sailed from Venice to Piraeus, sordidly and uncomfortably third-class in an Italian ship bursting at the seams with emigrants bound for Israel and disgruntled Cypriots returning home from places like Coventry. At the last moment one of Britain's recurrent currency crises had slashed our travel allowance to twenty-five pounds each. On this we had somehow to survive for two weeks until our return sailing-date. We stayed at a shabby hotel, unfashionably near Omonia Square, and subsisted mainly on omelets and chips. We scraped money for an overnight stay in Delphi and a few days at Nauplia on the Gulf of Argos, a place of exquisite colours – the sea sapphire, the Venetian ramparts honey-gold and hung with purple petals, the boats dazzling white with keels of red or blue or orange, and, dizzily high above the town, that incredible fortress of Palamedes, biscuit-brown against the Aegean sky, with its square loopholes, zigzag stairs, and galleries slanting down the precipice. We explored Argos and Tiryns, but lack of a pound or two deprived us of Epidauros and Mycenae, which had to wait for another time.

The following year Austria, by contrast, gave us the fleeting illusion of opulence. A Viennese publisher had brought out *Comrades for the Charter*, but the Austrian currency was still blocked. It seemed a shame not to spend the royalties in Austria. I felt no eagerness, however, to see a Russian-occupied Vienna. Could the money be collected at Innsbruck, in the French zone? I was assured it could. Still dubious, and armed with our full sterling allowance in case of disappointment, we took train to the Tyrol. The next morning we hastened to the bank. 'Three's too many,' said Marian. 'I'll wait on this bench.' Ten minutes later we were running back to her in wild elation. We not only had the fairy gold in wads of authentic-looking schillings, we had twice the amount we had expected. For the first time in our lives we felt free to eat and drink what-ever was on the menu, and to ransack the shops of Innsbruck and Salzburg on what seemed, after so many years of austerity, a positive spending spree. It is hard now to realise the thrill one got then not only from small extravagances but from any colour or variety in the most prosaic context. A gay red or blue towel was a discovery only less exciting than an embroidered blouse. I myself went home in a jacket of Harris tweed such as I had not seen at home for a decade. Poverty might be good for the soul, but a little contrast did no harm.

Certainly our unwonted euphoria did not blunt our other perceptions. To hear *Eine Kleine Nachtmusik* in Mozart's own city lost nothing by the previous consumption of a delicious cream-laden *Salzburger nockerln*. To saunter through Innsbruck's old arcades, comparing the exquisite wrought-iron signs; to take the miniature train up the Zillertal to Mayrhofen, as Lawrence and Frieda must have done during their runaway summer almost forty years before; to scramble up the track to the Krimml Falls; to see the jagged peaks of the Wilder Kaiser and the waters of Achensee, with its *Constant Nymph* associations so evocative to my generation – all these combined to make that April journey unforgettable.

It may seem odd that we still did not go to Italy. I think the distance deterred us, especially after the long train-journey to

Venice to embark for Greece – the Greek trip was exceptional, of course, just as there was another special reason for going to Austria. To repeat the overnight journey to Milan, and probably to places beyond, did not attract us. We did not start regular visits to Italy until some years later, when, with Jocelyn married, Marian and I felt our family responsibilities lightened and a new freedom to travel by air. So innumerable sights and experiences were postponed for us. It was to be a long time before we saw Federigo's palace at Urbino or, sitting in the garden of Cipriani's at Asolo after a mellowing Sunday lunch, the plain spread far below that Queen Caterina's courtiers, and Browning later, must so often have surveyed with such delight. The pellucid springs of Clitumnus near Assisi, the Colleoni chapel on the hilltop at Bergamo, the Teatro Olimpico at Vicenza, Placidia's little mausoleum at Ravenna, the Palladian villas along the quiet green Brenta, the grass-grown streets of Ostia, the solitary uplands of Calabria, the Sicilian garden in which Lawrence met the snake at the water-trough – these and other discoveries had to wait.

The foreign journeys we did make were usually in the school holidays at Easter. Summer was for places nearer home, walking holidays when we stayed in farms and guest-houses. We still had no car. I had never in my life felt the slightest desire to drive – a typewriter is almost the only form of machinery that does not intimidate me – and I only gradually realised that I had become a social phenomenon. I was a man who, while now able to afford a car, neither possessed nor desired one. Later, with the unforeseen decay of public transport, this was to become a serious inconvenience, but by then I knew that I had left matters too late. I was too old, too temperamentally unfitted, to join the juggernauts.

In the late nineteen forties and early nineteen fifties, however, it was still possible to get about in Britain by train or bus without being regarded as a second-class citizen. We were able to introduce Jocelyn to places of happy memory – Grasmere and Borrowdale, Nidderdale, the Quantocks in Somerset, with the cottage in Nether Stowey where we had lived before she was born – and to visit others just as fresh to ourselves. One of our first summer holidays took us to Ireland, which I had wanted to see ever since my English master, Garry Hogg, had fired me with his own enthusiam for J. M. Synge. Now at last, with a delighted thrill of recognition, I caught an echo of Synge's west-coast diction on the lips of a country waitress in a Dublin teashop: 'The Zoo does be open till six o'clock.'

Ireland was too good to be true. From the moment we arrived, off the night boat from Fishguard and some unconscionably early train, everyone talked as though on a stage. There was the masterful factotum of the village stores and Commercial Hotel at Rathdrum, where we sought shelter from the drizzle when the hotel taxi failed to appear. '*I'll* get the taxi, madam, now just ye sit down an' enjoy the tay. Ye've come for a holiday, *I'll* find the taxi, I'll set inquiries afoot, I have me sources of information – sources that you, madam, as a stranger in the town, could not possibly tap. Ye've come from Rosslare? Ye *can't* have come from Rosslare. The train's not in yet.' We convinced him at last that it had, and we had got out of it half an hour earlier. He was undismayed. And I fancy he took the whole credit when at last the pre-arranged hotel car arrived, tracked us down by local grape-vine, and swept us up the forest-clad valley of Glenmalure.

In Dublin we were able to visit the old Abbey Theatre, soon to be destroyed by fire. Then we went over to Connemara. As the train pulled out a boy bumped me in the corridor and apologised, only to be rewarded with a tirade from his elder sister. 'Ye've no need to "sir" him! Ye've no need to "sir" anyone, save it's a priest – ye're as good as they are!' I was scribbling throughout that holiday, capturing scraps of character and dialogue – but what English writer dared compete with the Irish on their own literary ground?

Connemara was worth the long train-journey and the fifty-mile bus-ride from Galway on to Clifden. It looked just like the posters: slate-grey lakes fringed with reeds and the Twelve Pins sticking up against the sky, blue and grey and gold, and cabins white-washed every spring, and donkeys everywhere. Only our little guest-house was sadly out of keeping in that alien, savage landscape. Not a weed in its formal garden, not a speck of dust indoors, everywhere gentility, embroidery, antimacassars, the smell of polish and the odour of sanctity, with crucifixes, Sacred Hearts in crude paper, and other devout decorations everywhere. It was a grimly virginal establishment – unlicensed, needless to say – in which even the double beds looked embarrassed.

With the success of *Tales Out of School* I knew that I had won my beachhead. I was, in my own area, an established writer. Provided I did not run out of ammunition in the shape of ideas, I could hold on indefinitely.

True, with the publication of that book, I was more than ever associated in people's minds with children's literature, whether as creator or as critic. That was something I had never meant, and I still struggled against it. I could not spare time or energy to batter at the theatre doors. Radio offered me a partial substitute. I found its technique easy, and could not understand why a pretentious mystique had grown up around it. It seemed to me that one needed only a knack for dialogue and the wit to remember that the listener could not see anything. There were no exits, entrances, scene or time changes to engineer. One could be generous with characters, crowds and the suggestion of spectacle. The word was almost everything, the writer supreme. In dramatising one of my own books I could lay the volume open by the typewriter and rattle off a script which the producer would put on the air with scarcely an alteration. Only once or twice, out of courtesy or curiosity, did I go to a studio rehearsal. I found radio drama a most congenial medium, but it did not pose the same challenge as the stage or completely satisfy the theatrical side of my nature.

I wanted also to get back to adult novels. But with the post-war transformation of the public library, turning the most prosperous reader from a book-buyer into a book-borrower, fiction was already beginning its economic decline. Several publishers were always ready to take another of my children's books. No one encouraged me to write a novel. My notebook reminds me that on 1 May 1949, during a Devon holiday, the main theme and opening sentence of *Snared Nightingale* flashed ready-made into my mind. It was six more years before I could afford time to speculate on writing it. I then waited with some tension for the reviewers to stick their knives in – the children's author entering the adult field is easy meat – but I was treated

generously. The *Times Literary Supplement* said I had 'achieved
a minor classic'. Nobody sneered or even patronised. Yet, such
were the conditions of novel-publishing even by then that
within a few years the 'minor classic' was out of print and
traceable only in public libraries, whereas my first children's
story was selling after a quarter of a century – and indeed still is,
as I write this, forty years after its publication.

Most tantalisingly, such 'children's' stories are widely read
by people, and quite critical people, of all ages. Since the craft
of storytelling fell into disrepute with reviewers of the so-called
'serious' novel, a surprising number of adults who obstinately
enjoy a well-told story have turned to the children's book,
which, itself vastly more sophisticated than the fiction of their
own youth, has come half-way to meet them and earned the
more accurate description of 'junior novel'.

Thus, in 1952, I had this letter from Sir Charles Trevelyan,
education minister in the Labour Government long ago:

> Your books are becoming such an important interest in our
> life that we want to let you know that there is a circle here
> where they are read greedily, whatever they are about. . . .
> There is not one of them which is not giving pleasure to me
> at the age of 80. . . . You have jolly good historical opinions
> and prejudices; but you never let your party views force the
> pace or get beyond truth. . . . My brother, the great historian,
> thinks that Scott did more for history than most historians. . . .
> I am writing this simply out of gratitude and in the hope that
> it will please you and spur you on to other adventures.

Thus began a heart-warming correspondence which continued until his death. He pressed me to visit him if I was ever
passing that way, but one is not always 'passing' Northumberland and it was some time before a Monday lecture-engagement
in Scotland gave me the chance to propose myself diffidently for
the weekend. The long-standing invitation was warmly confirmed. His secretary would meet me off the train at Newcastle.
A separate letter from Lady Trevelyan brought precise instructions on how to reach Wallington by bus. It occurred to me,
belatedly, that the house I was going to was in the stately-home

category and that left-wing politics were not always held to be
incompatible with social grandeur. Not knowing what to
expect, I dropped a hint that I planned to travel light. Sir
Charles took it. 'No such follies as dressing for dinner,' he
wrote back on a picture postcard, mischievously choosing a
view of the dining-table in the great balustraded hall, created a
century earlier at Ruskin's suggestion by roofing over the
courtyard round which the house was built. Sir Charles repeated
firmly that I was to look out for Miss Bulmer at Newcastle
station. She was there, and, as she drove me through the mellow
July countryside, I was able to reassure myself that my visit was
welcome. The old man had nearly died a month or two earlier,
but was better now and eager to meet me.

My host and hostess were in the library, Sir Charles twinkling and tweedy, Mr Punch turned country landowner, and
Lady Trevelyan astringently decisive and rather *grande dame*.

'I understand, Mr Trease, that you write boys' adventure
stories? So presumably you know the points of the compass? If
I tell you that this house is a perfect square, and that your room
is in the north-west corner, I need not show you to it, I am
sure.'

I was relieved when, going up half an hour later, I found
that Miss Bulmer had left my bag in the room where I hoped to
find it. At least I had successfully passed my navigation test.

It was an interesting weekend. We were alone in that great
house, built in 1688 on the site of a previous castle. Daily help
came in from the village – we dined amply that night on haggis,
preceded by artichokes – and Miss Bulmer appeared from her
adjacent cottage at ten o'clock sharp, when Sir Charles, who
was forbidden stairs, seated himself in a lightweight chair with
poles and I helped her carry him up to his room.

The next morning, a wet one, we drove through his beloved
but near-invisible Border countryside, Lady Trevelyan sitting
with me on the back seat, knitting diligently and pointing out
such landmarks as loomed dankly through the mist. 'That old
building was once an inn,' she observed disapprovingly, 'but
my father-in-law had it put down. Since when', she added with
evident satisfaction, 'there has never been a drop of liquor in
the village.' As I had noticed on the previous evening,

Wallington kept up a strong temperance tradition, and I felt it diplomatic to suppress the fact that I was the son and grandson of wine merchants.

We called on Sir Charles's younger brother, G.M., at Hallington Hall some miles away. The historian's sight was now very bad, and he told me he had to restrict his reading to about an hour a day. I glowed inwardly when he told me that some of this precious time had been spent on my stories, and when, a month later, I received a note in his shaky hand: 'I just wanted to tell you how much, since I saw you, I have enjoyed reading *Trumpets in the West* and *Cue for Treason*. The historical truth is admirable.' It is obvious, of course, why the Trevelyans approved of my stories, for my writing was much influenced by the G.M. tradition. I wish they could have lived to read my Garibaldi books, *Follow My Black Plume* and *A Thousand for Sicily*, in which my debt, formally acknowledged, was immense.

In the course of the weekend I became more at ease with my hostess. Sir Charles could entertain me only at ground level, reading aloud with tremendous gusto from his favourite *Border Ballads* and showing me the treasures of the library and his study, including the copy of Thucydides which his great-uncle Macaulay used to read each morning as he shaved. The stains of century-old lather still dappled the elegant Greek characters. For the rest of the house, and the distant walled garden, Lady Trevelyan was my indefatigable guide. We climbed to the attics, talking of her grand-children. I saw the four thousand toy soldiers with which Charles and his brothers had played as boys. We emerged on the roof and looked down on the grounds, the woods, the far-flung estate. There I took the bull by the horns and asked if I had been right to take up her husband's invitation. I had not known of his recent illness. Was my visit proving too much for him? Her warm answer reassured me. 'Can't you *see*?' she said – and her love for him flashed out, suddenly ardent, in her tone. 'He's loving every *minute*.'

I had to leave very early on the Monday to catch the Edinburgh train. 'No trouble,' she said. 'Sir Charles always sees the estate men at eight.' Over breakfast she said briskly, 'Just two things, Mr Trease. The visitors' book. . . . ' As I signed it, I saw that the preceding two guests – on separate dates – had been Hugh Gaitskell and Aneurin Bevan. 'Sir Charles feels much easier now', she commented, 'about the future of the Labour Party.'

'There was something else?' I reminded her.

'Yes. You are catching your train at Morpeth – a station I never use.' The last phrase was spoken in a dismissive tone that could have closed the line. 'I have some money due to me from the railway, but it has to be collected from the stationmaster there. Would you be good enough to do that for me, and let me have it at your convenience?' She passed over a printed card from Euston Station. It informed her, with reference to her claim for a seat-reservation not used, that the sum of one shilling, less threepence postage, would be refunded on application to the nearest station, Morpeth. 'I am not *mean*, Mr Trease,' she explained, 'but I was brought up to be *frugal*.' I took care to enclose ninepence in stamps with my letter thanking her for my entertainment.

All too soon, I was doubly grateful for the chance I had been given to meet my faithful and appreciative reader. He died quietly in his sleep six months later, and there were no more of those boyishly enthusiastic letters from Northumberland.

CHAPTER FIFTEEN

The Rock Bun Hills

ONCE we know that a writer is not going to die young in a garret, his biography loses interest unless he can fortify it with extraneous adventure or outrageous behaviour. By the 1950s I must have become the publicity man's despair. I was still happily married to the same wife, I did not make scenes in public places, I had no wanderlust driving me from one exotic foreign home to another.

On the contrary, I believed in roots. I wanted to put them down, finally. But where? During the war and just afterwards we had often discussed our next move – Abingdon had no claim on our affections and I found the Thames Valley in general too sleepy and inimical to work – but the 1950s found us still in the little house facing across the cornfields to the College. Like so many other respectable, responsible parents (which is exactly what we had become, and unashamedly) we were influenced largely by our daughter's education. Jocelyn was happy at Oxford High School, to which she travelled daily on the bus that passed our door, and for the rest it was not a bad environment for a girl to grow up in. She could ride in the surrounding fields and lanes – a young woman had a few ponies just down the road. There was swimming in the Thames at Radley. There were two theatres in Oxford, and we scarcely missed a play. So Marian and I agreed that, though we did not mean to end our days in Berkshire, it was a pity to disturb Jocelyn until her schooldays were over.

How can the autobiographer write of his nearest and dearest without embarrassment either to them or to the general reader? If he is silent, he leaves out much of the story he has set out to tell. If he lets his pen run on, he breaks confidences and shatters a privacy he has no right to destroy. So, though reticence is out of fashion, there is still a place for it, and this is the place. Life matters more than literature.

So far as my daughter is concerned providence has given me a way out of the dilemma. There is a vignette of her as a schoolgirl, not in the words of a fond father but in a cutting from the *Oxford Mail*. The dramatic critic at that time was S. P. B. Mais, a man I never met but one whose lyrical early novels, in the 1920s, had been a delight and a lasting influence upon me as a schoolboy. His criticisms of amateurs could be acid. So it was with some foreboding that Marian and I, on our way to the second performance of the High School's *Romeo and Juliet*, bought a paper and turned to his account of the first night.

> It was a real joy to see for once in Jocelyn Trease a Juliet of the right age, still in her early 'teens, unsophisticated, innocent, and certainly lovelier than any other Juliet that I can remember. Her beauty, particularly in the balcony scene and death scene, held me so much that I entirely forgot to listen to the words. Her voice was soft, sweet and low, her movements graceful and her emotional expression, whether of love or grief, simple, fresh and spontaneous. She was completely natural and delighted me especially by never trying to be more than the child she really is. I was deeply moved by her performance.

I have no similar convenient outsider's view of Marian. She had no taste for the spotlight. The back seat, not the platform, was her preference, and that known preference must shape even the phrasing of these very lines. Those curious must read *between* the lines. No writer, obviously, could have produced the sheer mass of work that I did in those years – whatever its quality – if he had not received the most devoted support. Marian kept the house quiet, packed me off on early trains, welcomed me home at midnight, held the fort in my absence, entertained expected and unexpected guests – American writers, B.B.C. producers, eccentric illustrators, old school-fellows, old army comrades, old pupils. She was the fuse-mender, the wielder of screwdriver and paintbrush. We shared tastes and interests and sense of humour ('but I *married* you,' she once said, 'because you made me laugh'), yet in other and convenient respects we were opposites and complementary. It would be quite inadequate to suggest that her contribution to my work lay purely in the provision of peace and quiet in which to do it. She read – or listened – to everything as it came, chapter by chapter from the typewriter. She pointed out accidental repetitions, slips, and ambiguities. Instinctively, like most creative people, I reacted impatiently to such criticism. But the seed of doubt was sown, and when I cooled down I nearly always saw that she was right and made the alteration. In the understanding of other people her observation helped me immensely, and that help had its effect on my writing. If my characters and their motivation carried any conviction, much of the credit was due to her.

By 1953 we were able to start thinking seriously of our move. Jocelyn had only another year at school. She already had a provisional place at Bristol, then the only university at which one could read Drama. We remembered the over-hasty way in which we had picked our home in Abingdon and meant to avoid that mistake. We could live anywhere if there were good trains to London and places where I might have to lecture.

The Lakes we had reluctantly rejected long ago. When I lectured there, people warned me of the long winter isolation. We wanted the best of town and country: Keswick, for all its superb setting, was too small. We took a January holiday at Brixham, the best season to judge a place for permanent living, and explored the coastal towns from Dartmouth back to Exeter. Noting the caravan-sites and other developments, we felt that the joys of spring would be outweighed by the horrors of summer. This would apply to the seaside generally.

At this point I read Anne Treneer's *A Stranger in the Midlands*, and if ever a book had a permanent effect on a reader's future life this one did. She wrote of weekends when she used to escape from the black-out and blitz of Birmingham and find peace walking on the Malvern Hills. I passed the book to Marian. 'Suppose', I said, 'we gave up any idea of the sea . . . ?'

I had been to Malvern only twice in my life, briefly and long ago. Marian had never been there at all. But I remembered that there were splendidly dramatic hills, miniature mountains, grander than anything else so near to London. The fame of the Malvern Theatre Festival still lingered – deceptively, as it proved, for the golden age of Bernard Shaw could never be recaptured, but we did not know that then. Map and railway timetable showed how central was the town's situation, how excellent the communications. These included through trains from Oxford, so it was easy to run over and see for ourselves.

The first time, Marian and I went alone. It was spring. The new fronds of bracken were pushing up eagerly from the thin soil that clothed some of the most ancient rocks in Britain. We strolled past the long frontage of a store, window after window displaying women's clothing. The number of windows seemed more appropriate to a big city than to a town of under thirty thousand inhabitants. And within a few hundred yards, sure enough, the last houses were falling behind, the road slanting uphill with unfenced common and young lambs peeping round the gorse. 'There you are,' I said, 'the best of town and country! Good shops and open hillsides, and only a quarter of a mile between them!'

That evening, describing our day to Jocelyn, Marian ended: 'And the hills go straight up out of the town. Like enormous rock buns.'

At half-term I took Jocelyn. We caught a bus to the foot of the British Camp, the Iron Age fort whose still-formidable ramparts and ditches girdle the table-top summit of Hereford-shire Beacon, eleven hundred feet above sea-level. We walked back to Malvern by the panoramic road cut to celebrate Victoria's Golden Jubilee, below the undulating ridge-line on the western side. Steeply below us lay the crumpled eiderdown of Herefordshire – apple-orchards, paddocks, copses, meadows, hopyards – stretching away to the low hill where Elizabeth Barrett rode as a girl, and behind it a little town where Mase-field spent his boyhood. But it was the horizon that caught our eyes: the majestic sweep of the Welsh Marches from the Sugarloaf at Abergavenny, along the escarpment of the Black Mountains, and on past Radnor Forest into those blue distances that inspired *A Shropshire Lad*. For, though the Malverns lie south of Housman's country, their western prospect is essentially his. At sunset especially it is Housman one remembers, not Masefield or Elizabeth Barrett or even Langland.

A thunder shower sent us scuttling to shelter in a church porch. Dazzling sunshine followed. We blinked into it, looking down over Colwall village below, chiefly aware of glistening railway lines and nursery greenhouses. 'There's one thing I know,' I said, 'I don't want to live *there*.' Words that I have since eaten, and with good appetite.

We now placed a regular order for the *Malvern Gazette*, to get an idea of the district. It had a woman editor, Joyce King, a fervent patriot who saw her adopted town as central to the universe. She was naïve, in turn impulsive and calculating, kind and unscrupulous, transparently and almost endearingly snobbish in her social values. The wife of the Council chairman was always reverently referred to as 'Malvern's first lady'. Joyce lived for the town and her paper, which faithfully reflected the world as she saw it. What mattered, she felt, were the great boarding-schools with their august heads and well-connected pupils (she dearly loved an ambassador's daughter), the gallant struggle to revive the famous theatre festival, the annual literary dinner, the Winter Gardens reception to visiting notables. . . . She was avid for praise of Malvern. Any overseas visitor, notable or not, was relentlessly tracked down, interviewed, and – provided his impressions were sufficiently favourable – chattily reported in the gossip columns. Her parochialism and self-confidence laid her open to amusing, and sometimes infuriating, gaffes – one used to open her paper in later years with a mixture of pleasurable anticipation and alarm – but when she died, suddenly and quietly in her office, something very individual was lost.

That was years later. Meanwhile, not unnaturally, our weekly study of her paper reinforced the favourable impressions we had ourselves already formed. More support came from an unexpected quarter.

I was lunching with David Davis to settle a radio commission. I remarked that we were now thinking of a move to Malvern. His face lit up. 'A splendid idea. I grew up there – my mother's still there. She might help you to find a house.'

My own mother was then much in our minds. She was

getting very infirm, she had given up the Nottingham house where I had spent my own boyhood, and her year was now split into four-month visits to each of her three sons. Climbing stairs had become difficult. We could make her more comfortable if we had a house large enough to allow for a bedroom on the ground floor. I said to Jocelyn, tentatively, 'Would it upset your last year at school if we made the move a bit earlier? I expect we could arrange – ' She did not let me finish. She knew she could stay with a school-friend in the Banbury Road. We need not worry about her at all.

So, early in the New Year, we wrote to house agents and to David's mother. Knowing that she, like my own mother, was about eighty, I thought she might be equally frail and did not expect much practical help from her. I imagined a deferential call upon an old lady and an amiable hour over the tea-cups. I was not prepared for the lively, humorous and delightful character who met us at Malvern station, swept us up under the noses of the waiting agents, and proceeded to drive us from one property to another in her 1930s car, driven with a certain 1930-ish insouciance with a preference for the middle of the road. But even her charm, and the hospitality she lavished on us at her early Victorian villa near the public library, could not dispel our disappointment. All the houses for sale were impossible. Either they were huge, unheatable, pretentious piles or they were mean and characterless, far inferior to our present home. We took the train back somewhat deflated.

Mrs Davis wrote urgently a few days later. She was sure she had found a house to suit us, if we were willing to spread our net a little wider and consider Colwall, just three miles over the hills on the western, Herefordshire side. But we must come at once. Someone else was after it.

Marian returned from an early visit to the town to find me already scribbling an explanatory note for Jocelyn when she came home from school. I passed her Mrs Davis's letter. 'We're catching the next bus into Oxford,' I said. 'We can lunch on the train and be in Malvern just after two. I'll phone the agent to meet us.'

It was an ideal day for unsentimental judgements. The agent drove us through swathes of wet mist. We crossed the ridge at

about nine hundred feet. On a clear day one can see thirty or
forty miles across the Welsh Marches, to Radnor Forest, the
Black Mountains and the upper reaches of the Wye, while
eastwards the Vale of Severn is spread at one's feet with the
long rampart of the Cotswolds beyond. That day we could see
nothing but the windscreen wiper.

We dropped steeply down into invisible Herefordshire,
turned several hairpin bends, branched down a curving side-
road, and pulled up on a corner in front of high, blank-looking
wooden gates. Ducking under dripping boughs, squelching over
drifts of sodden beech-leaves, we hurried up the drive and the
house itself loomed in front of us, embedded almost to its eaves
in glistening greenery, a secretive place. Later we learned that
for the previous thirty years hardly anyone had been invited
to cross the threshold. As we stood in the porch I said to
Marian, 'It faces south, so the hills must be over *there*.' 'I'll
take your word for it,' she said. Even the end of the garden was
lost in the shimmering veil of January rain. It was as well that,
in such a downpour, exploration was unthinkable. We could not
guess the extent of the garden, front and back, or the amount
of work involved.

The sad crushed widow opened the door and showed us
round. The interior was even darker than the day. There were
hideous wallpapers, one with a kind of purple cabbage design,
paintwork of excremental brown, a sink to shudder at, bedroom
wash-basins of antediluvian design and gas-fires of the same
period, though welcome enough as evidence that gas was
available in the village. But the proportions of the house were
good, the hall nobly wide for so modest a building, the stairs
broad and shallow, the windows generous, the wood and the
workmanship apparently good. The house had been built on the
eve of the 1914 war, the last year of the old standards of
quality, for a woman of individuality and relatively modern ideas.
Two friends, wishing to be close yet independent, had commissioned a pair of houses on an acre croft. We were looking
at the easterly one. The original two ladies had had a communi-
cating door through their bedrooms, now walled up and papered
over, and a handy little wicket gate through the garden-wall,
but this too, like the ladies, was no more.

With the eye of faith, if that eye were keen enough, one could see great possibilities in such a house. We drove back to Malvern. In the rear seat Marian and I squeezed hands silently. We had no need of private consultation. We knew. At the agent's office I wrote a cheque for the deposit, 'subject to contract'. Then we dashed to tell David's mother. She answered the bell herself and saw our radiance. 'You *haven't?*' she cried. 'O, Hallelujah!' And for all her eighty years she practically danced on her own doormat. An hour or two later, as our train stood in Worcester station, I leapt out and telephoned Jocelyn, already deep in her prep. 'We've bought a house,' I said as casually as I could. She gasped. 'Daddy! You haven't!' Everybody seemed to be saying that, but we had.

Nor ever yet regretted it. Ten years afterwards I learned that Anne Treneer was coming by herself to the eightieth anniversary dinner of the Society of Authors at Stationers' Hall. I arranged for us to be placed beside her, and at last we had the chance to meet her face to face and thank her for, unwittingly but so happily, influencing the course of our lives.

We moved in April 1954. It was a slow, cool spring, but our first weeks were dry and clear. We could see where we were, in every sense. The rock bun hills rose brown and green above the enclosing walls and hedges. Jocelyn's bedroom window framed British Camp, two miles away due south, flat-topped and stepped in outline like a Mayan pyramid. From the little east room, which soon became my study, I could see Worcestershire Beacon, the highest point of the range.

It was a sleeping beauty of a house, this house which I afterwards depicted almost exactly as Sandra's home, 'Apple Garth', in *The Maythorn Story*. It was too overgrown and had to be liberated. Climbing roses, japonica, firethorn and Virginia creeper pressed round its windows rampantly. It peered out at the world like an old English sheep-dog, purblind. The garden had too many trees, especially apples, some ancient and dangling bunches of mistletoe. It is the blossom I most remember from that first spring – not only the coral-red of the opening apple, but the cold white cascade of the cherry under the hall window, the snowy pear facing the dining-room, the brilliant japonica fanning out across the sandy-brown brickwork of the house, the neighbour's crab nodding amiably across the stone wall. Then came the lilacs, the curious laburnum, half yellow and half pink, the sweet-scented tree-peonies, the long hesitation and at last the sudden magical unfurling of the great copper beech. If the agent had promised us a quarter of all this on that first soggy January afternoon we should have discounted it as blatant sales talk. The garden was full of discoveries to be made. A season's neglect had already carpeted the stone flags so that I had to trace their whereabouts like an archaeologist, tapping the surface layer of rotted vegetation with the edge of a spade. There were cone-shaped yews and arbours to be trimmed back into shape, hedges tamed, balus-trades and urns and steps to be cleansed of their encrusting moss. Though I was never to find the satisfaction in gardening that Marian did, a new interest was certainly added to my life.

Even before our own labours began, the mere coming of spring had wrought an outward transformation to our purchase, and indoors an equally striking metamorphosis was in progress. David's mother had found us a joiner and decorator prepared to tackle any problem from roof to drains. Stuart Jones became a friend to whom we constantly turned. We dubbed him our 'Clerk of the Works' and he never let us down.

Before we moved in, he had already worked wonders. Light, and the colours of our choice, flooded the interior and banished its previous gloom. The old wash-basins had been replaced, the heavy mantelpieces skilfully changed or completely removed, the woodwork painted white, the walls papered with designs we had ransacked the London showrooms to find. Afterwards, year by year as his time and our funds permitted, Stuart Jones came back again and again to carry out this improvement or that. It was he who replaced the unwelcoming high wooden gates with wrought-iron ones that framed a glimpse of garden within. It was he who levelled a tiresome unwanted vegetable patch and paved it for Marian's rose-garden. It was he who built cupboards, bookshelves and a corner fitment which I designed for the television set. Wood was his first and abiding love, wood fashioned with old-style craftsmanship.

As the house had no outside wall to the west, it was hard to see how even Stuart Jones could give us a window from which to watch the A. E. Housman sunsets that were the common evening glory of our region. Then it occurred to me that perhaps the blank north wall of my study upstairs could be knocked out and a spacious bay thrust out on brackets, offering an expanse of glass on three sides that would frame the whole sky on summer evenings. Mr Jones tackled the practical problem with his usual zest. The bay was prepared in his workshop and duly fitted on cantilevers. It embodied a cushioned window-seat with a shelf below which comfortably housed my *Encyclopaedia Britannica*. That bay had an exhilarating suggestion of a ship's bridge. It rode high above the tossing foliage of the back garden and gave a view for miles.

So, at last I had my study. I had space – never space enough, of course, but who ever has? – for my lengthening rows of reference books, my filing-cabinets, transitory stacks of review-copies, clutter of notebooks, newsletters, learned journals, useful brown paper and all the other accumulation of a creative life. I had quiet, privacy, and yet, when needed, the refreshment of a window on the world.

Drawn by the clop of hoofs I could watch the riders filing down the Mathon road. Or the voice of a schoolmaster in apparent anguish would direct my gaze across to the playing-field beyond, where shrill and argumentative little boys tumbled and wrestled over a rugger ball, and I could thank my stars that my prep-school teaching days were far behind me. Or, thumbing through Roget for an elusive word, I had only to raise my eyes to West Malvern, high on the flank of the Beacon, to remind myself that there was the very village where the great verbalist compiled his thesaurus and now lay at rest.

Then it would be back to the typewriter, the phrases flowing again, mind refreshed rather than thread broken. Thus far from London there were few chances to dissipate time on parties, gossip and the seductive sociabilities of the book world. All the more enjoyable for that reason was the rare journey to London with the stimulus of talking shop to fellow-authors, publishers and radio producers. Equally welcome, for the same reason, was the arrival on the doorstep of visitors from that other world – David perhaps and his wife, Barbara Sleigh, complete with their Persian cats, returning from their house on the

Welsh coast, or Malcolm Saville *en route* for his beloved Shropshire, or some other writer, whether old friend, acquaintance or complete stranger, who had taken the trouble to track me down. In Colwall we quickly made interesting friendships. Our experience was quite different from that of Mazo de la Roche, who settled in the village for a year or two in the 1930s and loved the scenery but had no use for the people. Perhaps the people, like the world, had changed a good deal by the 1950s. We at least counted ourselves lucky – unforeseeably, almost undeservedly lucky – in dropping into a congenial community which we had picked, practically, by sticking a pin into the map. But naturally, in a profession as solitary as mine, an encounter with another writer had a uniquely tonic effect.

Such agreeable interruptions would always, in remote Herefordshire, be too rare to upset my steady working routine. Not until Jocelyn had married, and begun to provide us with granddaughters, was there any serious need to defend the privacy of the study. Then, before they could read even English, the girls had to learn the significance of the trilingual card they sometimes found dangling from the door-knob. I had filched it from a hotel in Madrid, I confess, because I found its wording irresistible in Spanish:

NO MOLESTAR
Ne pas déranger
Do not disturb

And behind that door – to conclude this book with much the same words as I began – I 'go on writing', for all my life I have had to write.

List of Books by Geoffrey Trease

NOVELS
Such Divinity, 1939
Only Natural, 1940
Snared Nightingale, 1957
So Wild the Heart, 1959

TRAVEL
Walking in England, 1935

HISTORY
The Italian Story, 1963
The Grand Tour, 1967
Matthew Todd's Journal
   (editor), 1968
Nottingham, a Biography, 1970
The Condottieri, 1970
Samuel Pepys and His World,
   1972

CRITICISM
Tales Out of School: a Survey
   of Children's Fiction, 1949;
   revised edition, 1964

PLAYS
After the Tempest (in Best One-
   act Plays of 1938)
Colony (unpublished, produced
   at Unity Theatre, 1939)
Time Out of Mind (unpub-
   lished, produced by the
   Repertory Players at the
   Comedy Theatre, 1967)

AUTOBIOGRAPHY
A Whiff of Burnt Boats: an
   Early Autobiography, 1971

For Young Readers

JUNIOR NOVELS
Bows Against the Barons, 1934;
   revised edition, 1966
The New House at Hardale,
   serialised 1934; book 1953
Comrades for the Charter, 1934
Call to Arms, 1935
Missing from Home, 1937
Mystery on the Moors, 1937
The Christmas Holiday
   Mystery, 1937
Detective of the Dales, 1938
In the Land of the Mogul, 1938
Cue for Treason, 1940
Running Deer, 1941
The Grey Adventurer, 1942
Black Night, Red Morning,
   1944
Trumpets in the West, 1947
The Hills of Varna, 1948
Silver Guard, 1948
No Boats on Bannermere, 1949
The Secret Fiord, 1949
Under Black Banner, 1950
Black Banner Players, 1952
The Crown of Violet, 1952
The Barons' Hostage, 1952
The Silken Secret, 1953
Black Banner Abroad, 1954
Word to Caesar, 1956
The Gates of Bannerdale, 1956
Mist over Athelney, 1958
The Maythorn Story, 1960
Thunder of Valmy, 1960
Change at Maythorn, 1962

Follow My Black Plume, 1963
A Thousand for Sicily, 1964
The Red Towers of Granada,
  1966
*The White Nights of St
  Petersburg*, 1967
Horsemen on the Hills, 1971
Popinjay Stairs, 1973

CHILDREN'S STORIES
*The Mystery of Moorside
  Farm*, 1949
The Fair Flower of Danger
  1955
The Dutch Are Coming, 1965
Bent Is the Bow, 1965
The Runaway Serf, 1968
A Masque for the Queen, 1970
A Ship to Rome, 1972
A Voice in the Night, 1973
The Chocolate Boy, 1974

TRAVEL
Red Comet, 1937
*The Young Traveller in India
  and Pakistan*, 1949
*The Young Traveller in
  England and Wales*, 1953
*The Young Traveller in
  Greece*, 1956

HISTORY AND BIOGRAPHY
Fortune My Foe, 1949

The Seven Queens of England,
  1953
Seven Kings of England, 1955
*Edward Elgar: Maker of
  Music*, 1959
Wolfgang Mozart, 1961
Seven Stages, 1964
This Is Your Century, 1965;
  revised edition, 1969
Seven Sovereign Queens, 1968
*Byron, a Poet Dangerous to
  Know*, 1969
*D. H. Lawrence, the Phoenix
  and the Flame*, 1973
*Days to Remember, a Garland
  of Historic Anniversaries*,
  1973

CRITICISM
Enjoying Books, 1951
The Young Writer, 1961

PLAYS
*The Dragon Who Was
  Different*, 1938
The Shadow of Spain, 1953

About the Author

Margaret Meek, *Geoffrey Trease*,
a Bodley Head Monograph, 1960